card

D0482718

tricks

galore

BOB LONGE

Sterling Publishing Co., Inc.
New York

Library of Congress Cataloging-in-Publication Data

Longe, Bob, 1928–
Card tricks galore / Bob Longe.
p. cm
Includes index.
Summary: Gives instructions for performing more than
thirty-five different card tricks of various types.
ISBN: 0-8069-2060-2
1. Card tricks Juvenile literature. [1. Card tricks.
2. Magic tricks.] I. Title.
GV1549.L527 1999
793.8'5—dc21 99–20303
CIP

3 5 7 9 10 8 6 4 2

Published by Sterling Publishing Company, Inc.
387 Park Avenue South, New York, N.Y. 10016
© 1999 by Bob Longe
Distributed in Canada by Sterling Publishing
℅ Canadian Manda Group, One Atlantic Avenue, Suite 105
Toronto, Ontario, Canada M6K 3E7
Distributed in Great Britain and Europe by Chris Lloyd
463 Ashley Road, Parkstone, Poole, Dorset, BH14 0AX, England
Distributed in Australia by Capricorn Link (Australia) Pty Ltd.
P.O. Box 6651, Baulkham Hills, Business Centre, NSW 2153, Australia
Manufactured in the United States of America

Sterling ISBN 0-8069-2060-2

CONTENTS

INTRODUCTION

Here you will find a wealth of card tricks of nearly every type, more than enough to provide you with several unique and diverse routines. The vast majority of these tricks have considerable spectator involvement, which, of course, insures greater interest.

Many of these are new tricks of my own invention. They are thoroughly tested and guaranteed to fool even the more knowledgeable. Others are old tricks of mine that I have dusted off and revised, using the basic principles to fashion fresh effects. As for the rest of the tricks, I have many friends to thank for their ideas and contributions, particularly Milt Kort, Wally Wilson, Ron Bauer, and Dave Altman.

I have tried to add something special to every trick in the book—original patter, a novel application, a surprise ending, better spectator participation, and so on.

Most of the tricks require no sleight of hand whatever. A few require a simple sleight or a special move. These can be quickly mastered by following the thorough instructions provided in the section *Some Important Moves.*

Be sure to give every trick a fair chance. In some instances, an easy, effective trick has to be explained at length, creating the impression that the trick is complicated. Run through *every* trick with a deck of cards to see if it's suitable for you. And be sure to consider ways in which you can improve each trick, thus making a particular effect exclusively yours.

Enjoy!

A FEW HUNDRED WORDS
OF ADVICE

It's hard to believe, but quite a few magicians do tricks for their own entertainment. If a spectator also happens to enjoy them, fine. But that's only incidental to the wonder the magician feels at his own superb ability. There's nothing wrong with this.

Some magicians prefer to show tricks only to other magicians, hoping to fool them with skill or a new principle. There is nothing wrong with this, either.

Both types of performers are missing the real fun of magic in which the marvel, wonder, and mystery of the trick are shared with an appreciative audience. The magician should not lord it over the group, but should be equally surprised. In effect, the magician is saying, "We're enjoying this together, and I'm just as excited about it as you are."

Don't misunderstand me. I occasionally show my tricks to other magicians. It can be fun and challenging. But you're unlikely to fool fellow magicians, and it's even less likely that they'll admit it if you do. A typical appreciative comment would be, "Very nice." If completely fooled, a magician might say, "Show that one to Joe," hoping, of course, to figure it out when you repeat the trick.

You should listen to and learn from fellow magicians, but be selective. Don't forget that some magicians have a fairly narrow view. For instance, I've heard some magicians complain, "There are too many four-ace tricks." What they really mean is that *they* have seen too many four-ace tricks. The average person has probably *never* seen a four-ace trick. Clearly, you can learn a lot from your fellow magicians, but try to remember that your primary audience consists of people who do not perform magic tricks.

You may have performed a trick a hundred times, but this audience has never seen it before. Don't be jaded. Try to bring the same enthusiasm to the trick as you had the first time you performed it. But with more skill, of course.

So, experiment, practice, and enjoy. We should all be performing for the fun of it, even when we're being paid.

SOME IMPORTANT MOVES

GIVE ME A BREAK

One of the more delicate moves in card magic is obtaining a secret break between cards, either with the left little finger or the right thumb. It's easy enough to do once you understand the concept. Because the secret break is essential to many trick moves, it's not a bad idea to master it.

First, let's consider the little-finger break. Usually, the idea is to obtain only a *small* break and to hold it with only the meaty tip of the little finger (Illus. 1). (In some instances, when doing advance sleights, the entire first joint of the little finger is inserted.)

Illus. 1

When a Card is Returned

How do you obtain this break? It depends on the trick you're doing. Let assume that you're fanning out the cards for the return of a chosen card. Fan cards from your left hand to your right, going through only a small portion at a time, limiting the replacement possibilities. The returned card and all the cards below it should be in a fairly neat pile in your left hand. All the cards above it are held loosely in the right hand. You slightly raise the right side of the cards in your right hand while closing them up. This gives you the opportunity to insert the tip of your left little finger just above the chosen card.

Below the Top Card
Suppose you wish to get a break below the top card of the deck. This can easily be accomplished one-handed. As your right hand is performing some sort of distraction, push the top card slightly off the deck with your left thumb. While drawing it back with the left thumb, insert the tip of your left little finger below it.

Below A Small Number from the Top
Suppose you want to get a break below a small number of cards from the top of the deck—for example, three. Find an excuse to fan out several cards from the top. It could simply be part of the trick you're doing, but, if not, you might say, "You can choose any one of these cards," or, "I can assure you that none of these cards is marked, at least not on this side."

As you fan the cards, let the right fingers rest on the bottom of the third card from the top. Just as when a card is returned, lift these cards slightly at the right side and close up the cards. While doing so, insert the tip of the left little finger below the third card from the top.

When Putting Cards on Top of the Deck
Let's say you're placing three cards on top of the deck, and you'd like to get a break beneath them. It doesn't matter whether you're putting them on top with the hand palm up or palm down. Simply put the tip of the left little finger in position just beforehand (Illus. 2). When the cards are placed on top, the break is taken automatically.

Transferring the Break to the Right Thumb
In nearly every instance, you'll want to transfer the break to your right thumb. This is almost automatic. Your right hand

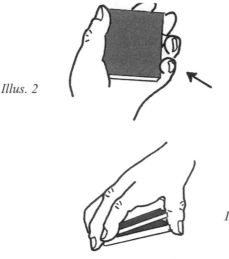

Illus. 2

Illus. 3

holds the deck palm down, fingers at the front, thumb at the back (Illus. 3). There is now no need to hold the little-finger break, for your right thumb now has it.

THE DOUBLE-CUT

This is a sneaky way to give the deck a complete cut. It is useful for bringing a selected card to the top or bottom of the deck, and in many other ways.

Suppose a spectator is sticking his selected card into the deck, which you are spreading out. Secure a break above the card with the tip of your left little finger. (See *When a Card Is Returned*, page 8.) If the card is to be cut to the bottom, get your break *below* the selected card.

Holding the deck from above in the right hand, transfer the break to the right thumb. (See *Transferring the Break to the Right Thumb*, page 9.) With the left hand, take a small group of cards from the bottom and place them on top, still retaining the break with your right thumb (Illus. 4). As you can see, you'll have to lift your right first finger a bit to allow the passage of the group to the top.

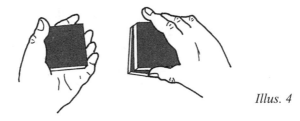

Illus. 4

Take the remainder of the cards below the break and place them on top. (To make the move even more deceptive, you might move three small packets from below the break instead of two.)

THE UP-AND-DOWN SHUFFLE

Hold the cards in the left hand in the dealing position. Push off the top card and take it into your right hand. Move your right hand forward (away from you) a few inches and push off the next card, taking it *below* the first one. You're now holding two cards. The top one extends about half its length beyond the lower card.

Move the right hand back to its original position and take the third card below the other two; it should be more or less in line with the first card. Move the right hand forward again, taking the fourth card below the others; it should be more or less in line with the second card (Illus. 5). Continue through the packet. When you're finished, hold the upper group with your left hand as, with your right hand, you strip out the lower group

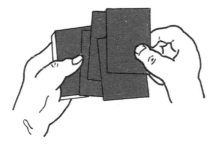

Illus. 5

from the others (Illus. 6). This group goes on top of the cards remaining in your left hand.

Illus. 6

Notes

(1) Depending on the trick, in the first move of the shuffle you may move the top card *down* or toward you, the next card up, the next card down, and so forth.

(2) Depending on the trick, when you strip out the lower group (the cards nearest you), these will sometimes go *below* the cards you hold in your left hand.

MILKING THE CARDS

Hold a packet of cards from above in your palm-down left hand, thumb at the inner end, first finger resting loosely on top, and the other fingers at the outer end (Illus. 7). Your palm-up right hand lightly grips the right side of the packet, thumb on top and fingers on the bottom. The right hand pulls the top and bottom cards to the right until they clear the packet (Illus. 8). The two cards are dropped onto the table. "Milk" two more cards and drop them on top of the first two. Continue until all the cards are in a pile on the table.

THE DOUBLE-TURNOVER FORCE

You know the name of the top card of the deck, and you wish to force this card on poor, unsuspecting Marilyn.

Say to her, "Let's have you choose a card. Please cut off a

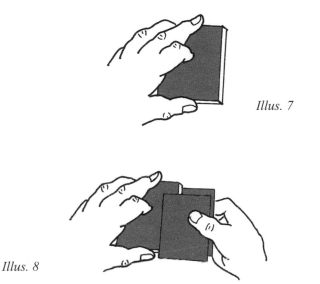

Illus. 7

Illus. 8

small pile." You hold out the deck so that she can take a small packet. "Turn that packet face up and set it on top of the rest of the deck." She does so.

Extend the deck toward her once more. "Now, Marilyn, please cut off a *larger* pile. Turn it over and set it back on top of the deck." She does so.

Fan through the face-up cards to the first face-down card. Hold the face-up cards, still fanned out, in your right hand. Thumb off the first face-down card onto the table, saying, "There's your card."

You have just forced the top card of the deck, using what is also called the "turnover force" or the "double-cut force."

AN EASY DOUBLE-LIFT

I am delighted to present an easy way of showing two cards as one.

First, you must hold a break beneath the second card from the top with the tip of your left little finger. (See *Below a Small Number from the Top*, page 9.)

You're about to lift off the top two cards as though they are one. With the palm-down right hand, grip the deck. The first finger is on top, the other fingers (at least the second and third fingers) grip the cards at the outer end (Illus. 9). The right thumb at the inner end takes over the break held by your left

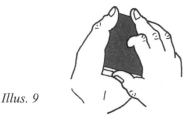

Illus. 9

little finger, as described in *Transferring the Break to the Right Thumb*, page 9. Casually, even the ends of the cards; actually, you're making sure that the first and second cards are perfectly aligned. Lift off the top two as one and show the face of the second card (Illus. 10). Return the double-card to the top of the deck.

Illus. 10

You now complete the trick. Incidentally, the most common trick is to place the top card into the middle of the deck and cause it to magically return to the top.

♣ LOCATION TRICKS ♣

DOUBLE DETECTION
(DOUBLE DE FUN)

Presenting a slick Stewart James trick. I have varied a few presentation points. The divination of the first card is from a trick invented, I believe, by Charlie Miller.

A strong feature of the trick is that you have excellent audience participation. You can have as many as four persons participate, or as few as two. In my description, I'll assume that you have managed to get four volunteers from the audience. They are Spectator A, Andrew; Spectator B, Beatrice; Spectator C, Caroline; and Spectator D, Dwight.

Go through the deck and take out a 10. Don't let anyone else see the card. Hand the card to Spectator A, Andrew, saying, "Here's a most important card. I'd like you to hang on to it for me. I want you to look at it and remember it, but don't let anyone else see it, okay?"

Hand the deck to Spectator B, Beatrice, saying, "Please give the cards a good shuffle. Then I'd like you to give a number of cards—say, fewer than ten—to this lady." Indicate Spectator C, Caroline. "And give the same number to this gentleman." Indicate Spectator D, Dwight. "When you're done, Beatrice, just hang on to the rest of the deck."

Make sure that all is understood, and then *turn your back*. Give Beatrice time to finish her chores.

Update: Andrew is holding a 10. Beatrice has given Caroline and Dwight the same small number of cards and is still holding the balance of the deck.

Speak to Caroline (Spectator C): "Caroline, please mix your

cards, choose one, look at it, and remember its name. Also, look at the back of the card and try to remember that as well. When you're done, place your card on top of the deck. Now place the rest of your cards on top of the deck."

When Caroline finishes, Beatrice is holding the deck, on top of which is a small number of cards, followed by Caroline's chosen card.

You'll recall that Spectator D's name is Dwight. Say to him, "Dwight, I'm going to face you guys again, so please hide your cards for a moment."

Turn back to the group and take the cards that Beatrice is holding (the main deck).

Andrew, Spectator A, is still tending his 10. Ask him to hand you the card, adding, "I need to put that card face up somewhere in the deck." Take the card, still not letting anyone see its face.

Put the deck behind your back with your left hand, and bring the 10 behind your back with your right hand. Put the 10 *face up* on top of the deck.

"While I'm at it, I might as well mix the cards a little."

Deal eleven cards from the top of the deck into your right hand, taking one on top of the other. Replace these on top of the deck. The reversed 10 should now be eleventh from the top. Bring the deck forward and either set it onto the table or hand it back to Beatrice.

Tell Dwight, Spectator D, to do the same as Caroline did— that is, shuffle his pile, look at a card and remember it, place it on top of the deck, and then place the rest of his cards on top of all.

You turn away while he does this.

Turn back, take the deck, and put it behind your back. "I'd better mix these a little." Give the ends of the deck a few riffles and then bring the cards forward. Naturally, the cards are still in the same order.

Caroline's card is eleventh from the top. "Let's see if you remember the back of your card, Caroline." Fan off four cards, studying the backs. "What do you think? No, none of those." Place the four cards on the bottom.

Fan off three more cards. "Do any of these strike you?" If she says yes, say, "Are you absolutely certain?" She can't possibly be, so you place these three on the bottom of the deck.

Fan off two cards. "Do you recognize the backs of either of these?" If she does, you must talk her out of it. You can try, "Are you *really* sure?" and similar questions. Ultimately, you might have to say, "Would you be willing to bet a thousand dollars on it?" Chances are, she'll say no, so you say, "Then you're not really certain." You place these two cards on the bottom of the deck.

You take off the next card and show her the back. "How about this one?" If she says, "That's it," say, "I know what you mean…it's similar, but I don't think so." Regardless, this card goes on the bottom also.

The next card is the one she chose. For the other cards, you hurried Caroline along, but now you're quite deliberate. Lift off the card and show Caroline the back. "How about *this* one?" If she says yes, fine. If not, say, "Think about it: Is it possible that this is your card?" Of course it's possible.

In either instance, say, "Good. Do you remember what was on the other side of your card?" If she doesn't get it, say, "You know, the name?" She names the card and you turn it over. "That's the one. Congratulations. I can't believe you were able to remember the back."

Hand Caroline her card or set it aside.

Have Dwight give the remaining cards one complete cut.

"Dwight, I'll bet you never even checked the back of your card, right? Then we'll just have to find your card the old-fashioned way. If you'll recall, I turned one card face up in the deck."

Turn to Andrew. "What was the name of the card I trusted to you?" He names it. Let's say it was the 10C. "As you recall, I stuck it somewhere in the deck face up."

Turn the deck face up and fan through until you come to the

one card which is face down among the face-up cards (Illus. 11). Place the cards that are in your right hand on top (the back) of the deck. "There's the card. Obviously, it's now face down. Let's make sure it's the 10 of clubs." Turn it over. It's the 10C, all right. "So the value of this card is 10."

Illus. 11

Place the 10 on top (the back) of the deck.

Say to Dwight, "Do you recall the name of your card?" He names his card.

You slowly count off nine cards aloud. As you say, "Ten," let everyone get a good look at the card now at the face of the deck. "And there we are, the tenth card is the six of diamonds (whatever)—your selection." Pause. Address the group: "If you've been holding the applause until the end, you can stop now."

Review

 (1) You give a 10 to Spectator A, asking him to keep its face hidden.
 (2) You give the deck to Spectator B, asking her to give the same small number of cards to Spectators C and D. You turn away while she does this.
 (3) With your back still turned, ask Spectator C to shuffle her cards, choose one, look at it, and place it on top of the main deck, which is held by Spectator B. She then is to place the rest of her cards on top of the deck.
 (4) After asking Spectator D to hide his cards, you turn around, take the deck, and place it behind your back.

Ask Spectator A to hand you the card you gave him. You take it without showing its face. Saying you'll put it face up into the deck, you place it face up on top. You then count 11 cards, one on top of the other, into your right hand. Replace these cards on top. Bring the deck forward and hand it to Spectator D.

(5) While your back is turned, Spectator D does exactly as Spectator C, as described in Number 3, above.

(6) You turn back, take the deck, put it behind your back, and give it a few riffles, presumably mixing the cards.

(7) Spectator C's card is 11th from the top. You have her study the backs of four cards, three more, then two, and finally one. She rejects all these, which are all placed on the bottom of the deck. She "chooses" the next card, which is turned over. This card is shown and set aside.

(8) Spectator D gives the deck a complete cut.

(9) You fan through the face-up deck to the face-down card that had been held by Spectator A. The cards you fanned go to the back of the deck. On the face of the deck is the face-down 10. You turn it over, showing it, and then place it also at the back of the deck. Spectator A names the card he had held. You then count down 10 cards in the face-up deck. Sure enough, the 10th card is the one chosen by Spectator D.

Note

I think you'll be surprised at how often the spectator will determine her card from the back. You show the first two groups of cards fairly rapidly; your attitude and your body language clearly say, "It can't be among these cards." You show the pair of cards with pretty much the same demeanor. And you still seem to be in a hurry. When you show the tenth card, you're getting a bit more positive, but you're still not sure. Most spectators pick up on these various signals and react accordingly.

When you show the back of the eleventh card, your attitude

changes. Don't go overboard, but be a bit more enthusiastic as you say, "How about *this* one?" More often than not, the spectator will say, "That's it."

A REAL FIND

The late Bob Hummer, a true eccentric, was ingenious at figuring out new magical principles and applying them. Here's an example.

As far as I can tell, in the magic fraternity this trick is always described incorrectly. It's almost as though the writers have never performed the trick. This is a shame since it's really excellent. I've tried to speed up the working and simplify the basic trick.

You'll need a complete deck of 52 cards.

You might start by explaining: "There's a certain lucky card in the deck that sometimes helps me locate a selected card. Let's see if it'll help me out this time."

Joyce always asks, "How did you do that?" so she'd be a perfect helper.

Hand her the deck and ask her to give it a good shuffle. Take the cards back and begin to deal them, one at a time, into a face-down pile. After you've dealt ten cards or so, say, "Stop me any time, Joyce." Meantime, you've been counting the cards. Suppose she tells you to stop after you've dealt off 18 cards. Remember the number 18.

"All right, Joyce. This is Pile 1. Obviously, I *could* know the number of cards here. So, when I turn my back, take some cards from this pile and hide them somewhere."

Push Pile 1 at least two feet to one side so that it won't get confused with another pile later on.

Set the balance of the deck onto the table and turn away. "Have you taken some cards from Pile 1 and hidden them? Good. We'll just forget about Pile 1 for a bit. Please pick up the rest of the deck, give it a good shuffle, and then cut it into two piles. Pick up either pile. Look at the card at the bottom of this pile. Show this bottom card around and remember it yourself. Now put this pile on top of Pile 1, which I pushed to one side. Pick up this combined pile. One other pile remains on the table. Pick this pile up and put it on top of the cards you're holding.

You turn back and take the deck. "Let's see if I can find my lucky card, and—maybe—your card." Actually, you can find the card quite easily, for you know what number it is from the top. I'll explain later. To perform the trick, all you need to remember is the number you dealt off at the beginning and the number 38.

In this example, you dealt off 18 cards at the beginning. So you start dealing cards fairly rapidly into a *face-up* pile. When you deal the first card, mentally count it as 19, the number after the one you're remembering. When you deal the second card, count it as 20. Continue adding one for each card dealt until you reach card number 38. At this point, you stop counting.

When you turn over the next card, say to yourself, "King." Turn over the next card and say to yourself, "Queen." Continue doing this in descending order. Suppose that when you mentally say a value—jack, for example— you turn over a card of that value. Let's say you turn over the jack of hearts. You say, "Here we have the jack of hearts. That's the lucky card I was telling you about. A jack has a value of 11. Let's see what happens when I deal off 11 cards."

You deal 11 cards more, counting aloud. The last card you deal is the chosen card. Stop, point to it, and say, "I believe that this is your card, right?" Right.

Incidentally, when you've dealt off about 30 cards, start slowing down, saying, "I think I'm nearing my lucky card." This enables you to do some thinking as you count down from king to ace. And, to improve the odds, you need a little time to think. For instance, you turn over a card and say to yourself, "Seven." The card, however, is the 8C, and 8 is one higher than your mental count. "Ah," you say, "the eight of clubs. My lucky card!"

You place the card face up back on top of the deck. "So let's count eight." You deal the 8 face up onto the pile, saying, "One." You continue to eight. Sure enough, the eighth card is the one selected.

Suppose the card you turn over is one lower than your mental count. You're mentally saying 7, but the card is the 6C. Again, it turns out that the 6C is your lucky card. You leave it face up on top of the pile you've dealt and then count off six cards from those you're holding. The *next* card is the chosen one.

Therefore, you want to take your time so that when you turn over a card, you can note whether it matches the number you're thinking of, or is the number before or after.

With the option of three cards with every card you turn over, it's clear that the odds are very much in your favor that you'll hit one. But if you don't, you still have a wonderful trick.

Now a wrinkle of my own. You've dealt off 38 cards and started a backward count from the king with the next card. Unfortunately, nothing matched—not even a match on either side of the value you turned over. You've counted all the way down to one, and the card you turned over is not an ace. The next card will be the chosen one. You turn it over, and say, "There it is—my lucky card." Look at the spectator with an inquiring gaze. "You look strange. Don't tell me that's your card, too." Sure enough, it is.

Note

How does this trick work?

Let's start with this point: If a card is two from the bottom, what number is it from the top? Obviously, 51. So if you know what number a card is from the bottom, and you want to find out what number it is from the top, simply subtract the number from the bottom from 53—*not* 52.

In our example, Joyce stopped you after you counted off 18 cards at the beginning. Let's suppose she removed no cards from the 18 but simply chose a card and put it on top of these

18. She then put the rest of the deck on top. Clearly, that card would be 19th from the bottom, or 34th from the top (53-19= 34). But what if Joyce had taken several cards from those 18 and had hidden them? It wouldn't matter; *the chosen card would still be 34th from the top*. And this is the crux of the trick that Hummer invented.

You can easily work out the card's number from the top. With this trick, as you've seen, you need not trouble yourself. You simply start counting with the number *after* the number you counted at the beginning. If you were to count to 52, you'd end up on the chosen card.

LET'S PLAY JACKS

In a "sandwich" trick, a chosen card is discovered between two significant cards, usually jacks. "Sandwich" tricks are always colorful and fun. This version by Al Leech is not only easy, but also extremely effective. I have revised the basic move slightly to make the trick even easier.

Take the red jacks from the deck and place them onto the table face up. Say, "The red jacks are real buddies. Generally, they like being together all the time. I'll try to prove that in a minute. But first, let's have Charles choose a card."

Charles selects a card. When he returns it to the deck, get a little-finger break above it. (See *When a Card is Returned*, page 8.) Bring it to the top of the deck, using *The Double-Cut*, page 10.

Hold the deck in position to perform an overhand shuffle, but with the faces of the cards toward the left thumb (Illus. 12). Ask Charles to pick up one of the jacks and turn it face down. "Charles, just drop it in here wherever you want. Just tell me when to stop."

Perform an overhand shuffle, taking several cards each time. The cards are landing in your left hand face up. When Charles tells you to stop, do so. Hold out the face-up cards that are in your left hand so that he can place his face-down jack on top.

Illus. 12

Put the face-up cards that are in your right hand on top of all.

Turn the deck face down.

"We now have a face-up jack in the deck. I'll show you." Fan down to the face-up jack. Fan past a bit so that you can get a left little-finger break beneath the card below the jack. (This move is identical to that used in *When a Card Is Returned*, page 8.) You're now holding a little-finger break below the chosen card.

Close up the cards and perform a double-cut, bringing the chosen card to the bottom of the deck.

Have Charles pick up the other red jack. "Turn the jack face up, please. Just tell me when to stop and drop it in."

Turn so that your left side is toward the group. You're about to perform another overhand shuffle, this time with the backs of the cards facing the left thumb, and you want to make sure that no one can see the bottom (chosen) card. As you shuffle this time, the cards land face down in the left hand. Charles tells you when to stop and drops the jack *face up* onto the face-

Illus. 13

down cards in your left hand. You drop the cards that are in your right hand on top of all.

The sneaky part is done.

"I promised that I could bring the red jacks together," you say, which is not quite true. "Let's see how I did."

Fan through the cards until you come to the red jacks with a card in between. "Whoops! What's this!" Take the three from the deck as a group. Make sure they are spread out, so that all can see them clearly as you display them. (Illus. 13). Put the three cards onto the table, still spread out. Set the rest of the deck aside.

Turn to the spectator who selected a card. "It looks as though someone's trying to break up their friendship. What was the name of the card you selected?"

He names the card. You turn over the usurper. Sure enough, that's the card

TRANSPOSITION TRICKS

INVISIBLE TURNOVER
This is a Roy Walton trick. I added a plot and got rid of a fairly difficult sleight.

You remove from the deck the K Q J of hearts and the J of diamonds, tossing them face up to the left on the table. Say, "There's a country called Deck o' Playing Cards—sometimes, just Cards. In the country of Cards, there's this royal family—the king, the queen, and their two sons."

When performing the trick, the order of the four cards doesn't matter. But to make it easier to follow the explanation, place the KH face up on the table first. On top of it, place the QH. Follow this with the JH and then the JD.

Since the cards are face up, it makes sense to say, "As you can see, the members of the royal family are really 'up.' And why shouldn't they be?"

Toss out five black spot cards face up to the right on the table. Use black 6's, 8's, and 9's. Again, the order doesn't matter, but for purposes of our example, place the cards into a face-up pile in this order: 6S, 8S, 8C, 9C, 6C. The face-up card on top is the 6C.

Pick up the pile and spread out the cards so that all can see them.

"These are the common people, the hoi polloi, the riff-raff—the people I can identify with. Sometimes they're 'up.'" Indicate with an upward gesture that they are face up. Close up the pile, turn the pile over, and spread out the cards again. "And sometimes they're 'down.'"

Turn over the second and fourth cards from the top (Illus.

14). "But usually some are up and some are down." Close up the pile, *turn it over*, and place it onto the table.

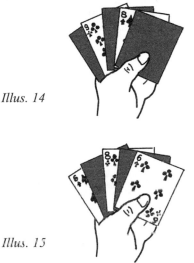

Illus. 14

Illus. 15

Now the first, third, and fifth cards from the top are face up. (If you were to pick up the pile and fan out the cards, they would be as shown in Illus. 15.)

"The same is true of the royal family," you say, picking up the face cards and spreading them out. "Sometimes they're up." Turn the cards face down and respread them. "And sometimes they're down." Turn over the first and third cards from the top (Illus. 16). "But, just like the commoners, usually some are up and some are down." Close up the pile, *turn it over*, and place it onto the table.

Illus. 16

"As you must know, very seldom do the royal family and the commoners get together. But in the land of Cards, once a year they all congregate for a square dance." Making sure you don't spread any of the cards, pick up the pile of spot cards and place it on top of the pile of face cards. As you do so, pick up the combined pile.

Turn the pile over so that the face-card set is on top. (See Illus. 17 for the position of the cards from top to bottom at this point. The shaded cards are face down.)

Illus. 17

Carefully, spread out the face cards that are now on top of the packet so that four cards are displayed, the first and third being face up (Illus. 18). Make sure you do not reveal the fifth card from the top. With your right hand, take out the third card from the top, turn it over, and return it to its original position from the top. Also with your right hand, turn over the top card. As you do this, say, "The royals will stand on one side of the hall, all facing the commoners."

Turn the entire packet over. As before, spread out the top three cards, turn over the third card in place, and turn over the

Illus. 18

top card. This time, be absolutely certain that you do not reveal the fifth card from the top, for this would expose the entire trick. As you turn these cards over, comment, "And the commoners stand on the other side of the hall, all facing the royals."

Pause. "And then they begin to dance!" You must now turn the pile over an even number of times. Turn over the pile once. Then turn it over two more times, saying, "Round and round they dance!" Turn the pile over three more times, saying, "Yes, round and round and round they dance!" You have turned the pile over six times. But the handling makes it difficult for spectators to tell the exact number.

"One time, after dancing for two hours, the royal family walked out to get some air." Deal the four top cards face down onto the table, about a foot forward.

You're holding five cards in your left hand. Spectators see a black spot card, which seems to be the first of the face-up spot cards. Make sure you don't move this fifth card; if you do so, you'll reveal a face card and spoil the climax.

"The commoners thought the royals had left for good. They decided to send a representative to ask them to return." You're holding the packet of five cards. Turn it face down. Shuffle the bottom card to the top of the packet in an overhand shuffle, making sure no one can see the faces of the cards. In doing this shuffle, simply make sure you shuffle the last few cards one at a time. Address a spectator: "Why don't you choose the representative? Which do you choose, left or right?"

The answer doesn't matter. You'll always start by dealing a card to your left and the next one to your right. (If the spectator chose right, the first card dealt will be on *his* right. If he chose left, the first card dealt goes on *your* left. You don't explain this; you simply start by dealing a card to your left, and then a card to your right.) Deal a card on top of the one on the left, and another on top of the one on the right. Place the last card on top of the cards on the left.

Pick up the three-card pile on the left. Deal the top card to the left, the next card on top of the two-card pile on the right, and the last card on top of the card on the left.

Pick up the two-card pile on the left. Deal the top card to the left and the other card on top of the three-card pile on the right.

Pick up the card on the left. It's the same black card that showed when you presumably dealt the royals on to the table. Briefly show its face, saying, "So you chose this fellow to go outside and talk to the royals." Drop the card face down onto the forward cards—the presumed royals. "But when he got outside, he discovered that all the other commoners had got there before him."

Turn over all the spot cards.

Pick up the four royals. "And the royals said, 'Come on back in; the dance has hardly started.'" Turn over the four cards and spread them out.

After a brief pause, pick up the spot cards and add them to the royal cards so that all the cards face the same way. Give the cards a little shuffle as you sadly comment, "But that was only once a year."

SPELLING EXCHANGE

Some time ago, I developed this trick in which, with little effort on the performer's part, a sort of transposition occurs. Some fine tuning was required, however. Recently, I made a few changes and ended up, I think, with a much better trick. So, for the first time anywhere, here it is.

Hand the deck to Mark and ask him to give it a good shuffle. As he does so, say, "I'd like you to think of a number from one to ten, Mark. Then I'm going to count the cards from the face-up deck so that you can see what card lies at your number. When I do this, I'd like you to remember both the card *and* your number."

When Mark returns the deck to you, turn it face up. Let's suppose that the card at the face of the deck is the 7S.

"Look at that, the seven of spades. I can't believe it. That's my lucky card, so we can't use the seven of spades as part of the count. So let's all forget about the seven of spades."

Fat chance, after you've mentioned it three times.

"Have you thought of a number from one to ten, Mark? Good. Now remember the card that lies at that number."

To be on the safe side, you may ask Mark to whisper his number to another spectator.

Take the card at the face of the deck (the 7S in our example) face up into your right hand. "Now we don't count this one." Take the next face-up card *on top* of it, saying aloud, "One."

Continue counting and dealing until you reach the count of 10. In your right hand, you're holding a pile of 11 face-up cards, the lowermost of which is the 7S.

"Because you shuffled, there can be no special arrangement of the cards, right?"

Start fanning cards from your left hand so that they go *beneath* those you're holding in your right hand (Illus. 19). Ostensibly, you're showing that there is no arrangement of the cards. Fan them one at a time, mentally spelling out the card which you claimed as your lucky card—in our example, the 7S. Move one card below the packet in your right hand for each letter in the spelling. Do not, however, include the final S in the spelling. In our example, you would transfer one card for each of these letters:

S-E-V-E-N-O-F-S-P-A-D-E

Note once more that you do not include the S at the end.

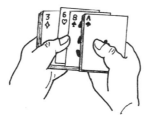

Illus. 19

Hold the cards that are in your right hand separate from the others. Make eye contact with Mark, saying, "Do you remember your card?"

As you say this, place the cards in your left hand on top of those in your right. Turn the deck face down.

Or you can do this: Again, hold the cards in your right hand slightly apart from the others as you spread out several more cards. Place the cards in your right hand on top of those in your left hand. In the process, take a break with the tip of your left little finger beneath the right-hand bunch. (See *When Putting Cards on Top of the Deck*, page 9.) Now with the cards still face up, perform a double-cut, bringing the original right-hand group below the other group. (See *The Double-Cut*, page 10.) Turn the deck face down.

"Don't forget, the deck was shuffled. Our job now is to see if we can find your card. Do you remember your number, Mark? What is it?"

He tells his number. You deal that number into a face-down pile. Turn over the last card you dealt. "That isn't your card, is it, Mark?" No. "Good."

Turn the card face down onto the pile. Place the rest of the deck on top of the pile. Pick up the deck.

"How are we going to find your card? Maybe we can use my lucky card. Does anyone remember what it is?"

You're told that it's the 7S. You spell out "seven of spades," dealing one card into a pile for each letter in the spelling. Lift off the last card you dealt and place it in front of Mark.

"What was your card, Mark?" He names it. You ask him to turn over the card in front of him. That's the one, all right.

As he turns the card over, you pick up the cards you just dealt off and put them on top of the deck.

"I tell you, it's a miracle. Now what was the number you thought of, Mark?" Again he tells you. You deal that number into a pile. Tap the last card you dealt off, and then turn it over.

"Ah, just as I thought—my lucky card!"

PREDICTION TRICKS

TWO FOR ONE

Martin Gardner and Bill Simon developed a trick called "Seven Outs." In trying to improve the trick, I developed a snappy version which is somewhat different. My experiments led to a *second* trick which, I believe, is superior to the original—at least in some respects.

Both tricks are predictions.

Version One

Ask Louise to shuffle the deck. When she finishes, take it back and fan through from the top, saying you're looking for a prediction. Note the card that's third from the top. Find its mate (the card that matches it in color and value) and set it aside face down, announcing that this is your prediction.

If you can, give the cards a false cut or a false shuffle. Instead, you may decide to use a slight variation of *The Double-Turnover Force*, on page 12. Louise cuts off a small pile from the deck, turns it over, and replaces it on top. She then cuts off a larger pile, turns it over, and replaces it on top.

You fan through the face-up cards, saying, "Let's begin with where you cut." Set all the face-up cards aside in a pile. Turn this pile face down so that the card at its face won't be a distraction.

Whether you did a false cut or *The Double-Turnover Force*, at this point you're holding the original top portion of the deck, and the card matching your prediction is still third from the top.

Hand this packet to Louise, saying, "Louise, what do you consider a lucky number?" Chances are she will say 7. If not, say, "I prefer 7. So please deal seven cards into my hand." Hold one hand out palm up.

She deals seven cards face down into your hand. The original third card from the top is now third from the bottom, or fifth from the top. Set the packet *face up* onto the table, saying, "I'd like you to choose a number from one to ten. We'll spell out the number that you select. Take your time and make sure you pick a number that you like." You may add a few more comments to provide additional time misdirection; you don't want to set the packet onto the table and then immediately pick it up again.

The numbers from one to ten can be spelled out in three, four, or five letters. Numbers one, two, six, and ten spell out in three letters; four, five, and nine spell out in four letters; and three, seven, and eight spell out in five letters.

If Louise designates a number that can be spelled in three letters, pick up the face-up packet with your right hand and place it, *still face up*, onto the left palm. Spell out the three-letter word from the face of the deck, dealing one card from the top onto the table for each letter in the spelling. On the table you now have a packet of three face-up cards. Lift off the last card dealt and place it, *face down* next to your prediction.

If Louise chooses a four-letter number, pick up the packet with your right hand and place it *face down* onto the left palm. Spell out the four-letter number, forming a face-down pile. Lift off the card that is *now on top of the balance of the pile* and place it, still face down, next to your prediction card.

If Louise selects a five-letter number, again turn the packet face down as you pick it up and place it in your left hand. As with the four-letter number, place each card face down as you spell. When you complete the spelling, pick up the last card you dealt and place it face down next to your prediction card.

In all instances, set aside the rest of the packet.

Don't immediately show the match between the spectator's choice and the prediction card. First, say, "You shuffled the deck. I placed the prediction card down long before you chose your number. Let's see if we have a match." Turn both cards over simultaneously.

Version Two

As with Version One, you announce that you're going to make a prediction. Fan through the cards from the top, noting the card that's *sixth* from the top. Find its mate and place it face down onto the table as your prediction.

You now follow the exact procedure described in the previous trick, as you perform *The Double-Turnover Force*. (In cutting off the smaller pile, Louise must cut off more than six cards, of course.) After the second cut, you set aside the face-up cards, turning them face down.

Say to Louise, "I'd like you to choose a number—say, 5, 6, 7, 8, or 9—your choice."

She names the number. In each instance, you will deal cards *onto the face-down packet on the table*. As you'll see, this doesn't matter for the first two instances, but for the other three, it makes all the difference.

If she chooses 5, deal five cards onto the pile on the table. Deal the next card face down next to your prediction.

If Louise chooses 6, deal six cards onto the pile on the table.

When Louise selects 7, 8, or 9, you want to make sure that the sixth card down ends up on top of the pile. So you follow a similar procedure for each number.

If she selects 7, push two cards off the deck, retaining their order. Take them into your right hand and set them face down onto the pile on the table. As you do so, say, "Two." In the same way, push off three cards, making sure all can see the number. Place them onto the pile on the table, saying, "And three is five." Push off two cards and place them onto the pile, saying, "And two is seven."

If she chooses 8, you first take two cards off, then three, and finally three more. With the first group, you say, "Two." Then you say, "And three is five." Finally: "And three is eight."

If Louise chooses 9, you remove piles of two, three, and four. As you remove the groups, you say, "Two. And three is five. And four is nine."

When she chose 5, the sixth card went right next to your prediction card. In the other instances, the top card of the pile on the table is the original sixth card from the top.

Whatever her choice, you now use some "time misdirection." Chat for a moment, explaining that the deck was shuffled, that you did not change the position of any cards, that Louise cut the cards, and that she had complete freedom of choice.

If she chose any number but 5, you now pick up the top card of the pile on the table and place it next to your prediction card.

As with Version One, reveal that the prediction and the chosen card match.

OLDEST TRICK IN THE BOOK

I recently developed an extremely deceptive prediction trick which spectators found most convincing. Examining the trick, I found that the main principle involved was quite familiar. In fact, it is the key to one of the oldest and simplest tricks ever: A spectator's card is brought to the top of the deck. The magician asks the spectator to name a number. The magician deals down to that number. Unfortunately, the chosen card isn't there. The cards are replaced on the deck. The magician says the magic words and counts down to that number again. Naturally, the chosen card is there.

As I started working on my effect, I didn't realize I was borrowing from an ancient trick. This was fortunate, I think, because I proceeded to develop the present trick in which the basic principle is completely disguised.

You commence: "I'll need three volunteers to help me with an experiment."

Abigail, Bruce, and Carl (A, B, and C) volunteer.

"I'm going to make a prediction," you explain. "Then you three will choose a card completely at random. First, let's have the deck shuffled."

Have Abigail shuffle the cards.

"I'm sure everyone here is wondering if one or more of you will try in some way to help me. We're going to prevent any possibility of that. We'll have Abigail choose a small number—a number from one to five—and take that many from the deck. This number I'll refer to as the 'fairness factor.' While she's doing this, Bruce and Carl will have their backs turned, so that they'll have no idea of what Abigail's number is."

Have Bruce and Carl turn their backs. "Abigail, please quietly count into a pile five or fewer cards."

She does so. Let's suppose she deals four cards. Without being too obvious about it, you count the number that she deals.

Take the deck from Abigail. "Hide the cards, Abigail, so Bruce and Carl can't see the number."

Turn to the two men. "Carl, please keep your back turned. Bruce, I'd like you to turn around now and think of a number from, say, 7 to 15."

Start to hand the deck to Bruce, but stop as you catch yourself. Laughingly say, "Just a minute…I haven't made my prediction yet. Let me think." Concentrate for a moment. Then start fanning through the cards *from the top of the deck*, the faces toward yourself.

Abigail chose a small number which she dealt into a pile. You *add one to this number* and note the card that lies at that number from the top of the deck. In our example, Abigail chose the number four. You add one to this, getting five. So you note the fifth card from the top.

Without pausing, continue fanning through the cards until you come to the card that matches it in value and color. Suppose that the fifth card from the top is the 6S. You fan through the deck until you come to the 6C. Remove this from the deck and place it face down onto the table, declaring that this is your prediction card. If the 6C is among the first four cards, just remove any other six.

Close up the cards and hand them face down to Bruce.

"Bruce is going to quietly deal into a pile a number from 7 to 15. Carl will have no idea of how many Bruce deals. Bruce, be sure to remember how many cards you deal; that's important."

Bruce deals a number of cards into a pile. Let's suppose he deals out eight cards. In our example, the card you noted, the 6S, is now fourth from the top in the pile Bruce dealt. You take the deck back from him.

"Carl, it's your turn. Please turn around and deal into a pile a number from 7 to 15. Be sure to remember the number." Hand him the deck. Suppose he deals 13 cards into a pile.

Take the deck from Carl and set it onto the table.

Without comment, pick up the pile that Bruce dealt and place it on top of the deck. Address Abigail: "Which pile should go on next, yours or Carl's?"

It really doesn't matter. The "fairness factor" pile and the other pile go on top in any order. Let's say that Carl's pile of 13 cards goes on top first. The 6S is now 17th from the top of the deck. And when Abigail adds her pile of 4, the 6S becomes the 21st card from the top. If Abigail were to add her pile first, the 6S would still be 21st from the top.

Pick up the deck. "We'll now count down to select a card. We'll not use Abigail's number, because that would completely negate the 'fairness factor.' What's your number, Bruce?"

He tells you, and you deal eight cards into a pile. Place the rest of the deck on top of the cards you dealt out.

"And what's your number, Carl?"

He tells you, and you deal 13 cards into a pile. You pick up the last card dealt—the 6S in our example—and place it face down next to your prediction card.

Put the deck on top of the remaining cards that you dealt. Everything is really tidy now. The chosen card and the prediction card are next to one another, face down on the table, and the rest of the deck is in a neat pile nearby.

"It's unlikely to work out, but if we've been unusually lucky, these two cards will match each other in color and value."

Turn the two over, showing that you have been extraordinarily lucky.

Review

(1) Get three spectators to help out.

(2) While the other two spectators turn their backs, Spectator 1 deals from one to five cards into a pile and hides them. You take note of the number.

(3) You choose a prediction card: Add one to the number chosen by Spectator 1. Fan through the deck and note the card that lies at that number from the top. Continue fanning through the deck until you find the mate to that card. Remove the mate as your prediction card and place it face down onto the table.

(4) Spectator 3 keeps his back turned as Spectator 2 deals from 7 to 15 cards into a pile.

(5) Spectator 3 now deals from 7 to 15 cards into a pile.

(6) You place Spectator 2's pile on top of the deck, followed by *the other two piles*.

(7) You deal out Spectator 2's number, followed by Spectator 3's number. The last card dealt out is the chosen card. You place it face down next to your prediction card. You turn them both over. They match.

MENTAL TRICKS

THE UNKNOWN NUMBER

Here is an updated version of a trick I invented many decades ago.

Oscar is willing to help, so you hand him the deck and turn away. You provide these directions with appropriate pauses: "Please shuffle the deck, Oscar. Cut off a fairly good-sized group of cards. (This ensures that the group will be higher than 10 and, preferably, higher than 19.) Count the cards that you just cut off. You now have a two-digit number, right? Add these two digits together. Don't tell me your total. But count that many cards back onto the deck. For instance, suppose you cut off 24 cards. You have two digits—the 2 and the 4. Add these two together, getting 6. So you'd count six cards back onto the deck."

Give Oscar some time to accomplish this. "Now push the deck to one side; we won't be using it any longer. You're still holding the rest of the cards that you cut off. From this group take some cards—say, fewer than 10—and put them into your pocket."

Turn back and take the remainder of the cut-off cards from Oscar. Fan through them, letting all see the faces, as you say, "Let's see what face-cards you have here." Inspect the group carefully. If there are face cards, pull them out and comment on each one. You might say, "Oh, yes, the jack of spades. Very significant." If there are no face cards, you could say, "Just as I thought—no face cards." Actually, you count the cards. Reduce the total to a single digit. For instance, if you count 13 cards, add the 1 and the 3, getting 4. Subtract the single digit from 9. This gives you the number of cards that Oscar has in his pocket.

In our example, you subtracted 4 from 9, getting 5. You announce the number. But not immediately. You might say something like, "I have the king of spades, which means that you have an odd number of cards in your pocket, Oscar. And this jack of hearts indicates that it's a fairly low number. I'd say that you have five cards in your pocket."

And if there are no face cards among those you hold, you could say, "No face cards at all, Oscar. That means that you have an ordinary number of cards—probably five. Yes, I think you have five cards in your pocket."

Notes

(1) The trick will work when the spectator cuts off any number of cards from 10 to 51.

(2) Suppose you're looking through the packet, presumably looking for face cards, but actually counting, and you find that the packet contains 18 cards. You add 1 and 8, getting 9. You subtract 9 from 9, getting zero. This means that the spectator has 9 cards in his pocket. It's possible that a smart aleck might put *no* cards in his pocket. I've never had this occur, but if it did, I would first announce that he had nine cards in his pocket. If he said no, I'd tell him he had zero cards in his pocket. And perhaps make a sarcastic comment about his choice.

PERFECT MATCHUPS

It's a rare trick indeed which you perform and *still* can't believe that it works. This astonishing Dave Altman concoction is just that. The original trick involved cards used for ESP testing. In my variation, ordinary playing cards are used.

Start by removing from the deck all face cards, tens, and aces, explaining, "We'll need all the high cards. The lower cards just don't seem to work out."

Set the rest of the deck aside. Fan out the high cards, holding them with the faces toward you. "Let's make sure I have them all."

Take out any ace and place it face down onto the table. On top of it, place a face-down ten. Follow this, in order, with a face-down king, jack, and queen. From the bottom up the order is this:

A 10 K J Q

It might help to remember the order this way: highest, lowest; next-highest, next-lowest; middle.

On top of these five cards, place three more sets in precisely the same order. Even up the packet and have it given at least two complete cuts. These cuts do not change the basic order, of course.

Illus. 20

"I think we have a pretty good mix here." Pick up the packet and hold it with the faces toward the spectators. Fan off three cards from the top. Take them into the right hand and display them so the spectators can see the faces (Illus. 20). Close up the fan and place the three cards *in front* of the cards in the

Illus. 21

left hand. In other words, place them on the bottom of the packet (Illus. 21). Fan out three more cards, show them, close them up, and place them on the bottom. Continue until you've shown all the high cards. Keep count of the number of packets and stop after you've shown seven sets. (One card will have been shown twice.)

An alternate procedure is to fan off three cards from the top, show them, and put them face up onto the table. Deliberately avoid looking at the faces. Show another set of three and place it face up on top of the first set. Continue through the rest of the packet. The last set you show will contain only two cards.

Showing the cards in either of the ways described tends to disguise the setup. Regardless, set the packet face down onto the table and have it given another complete cut.

Jim isn't busy, so ask him to help out. Continue, saying, "Jim, I'd like you to cut off as many cards as you want from this packet."

Chances are that Jim will cut off about half the packet, but it doesn't really matter.

"If you're not satisfied with where you cut, Jim, you can put those cards back and cut some off again."

When Jim is satisfied, continue: "You have those cards, and I have the cards you left. Let's each deal our cards like this."

With your pile, you demonstrate "milking" the cards. (See *Milking the Cards*, page 12.) If, at the end, one card remains in your left hand, place it on top of the tabled cards.

Go slowly, demonstrating, so that Jim can see exactly how to do it, forming his own pile on the table. If, however, he can't seem to get it, take his packet and "milk" it, forming the pile for him.

Let's assume, however, that Jim does it perfectly.

Set the packets side by side. "Jim, the cards were cut several times, and then you cut off as many cards as you wanted. We milked both packets. Now let's see if anything magical has happened."

Turn over the top card of each packet. Show that the cards

Illus. 22

match in value. Set each card, face up, *above* its packet, from your view (Illus. 22). Continue until one packet is exhausted. (Occasionally, the packets are even, and, of course, they run out simultaneously.) If one packet remains, pick it up and hand it to Jim. "Please milk the top and bottom cards, Jim." When he does so, have him turn the two face up. They match in value. Have him continue until all the cards are gone, and all the matchups have been shown.

DOUBLE DEALING

So-called "self-working" card tricks are plentiful, but are sometimes tedious or unremarkable, or both. Rarely does one come along that's clever, interesting, and deceptive. Here we have one, however. I have no idea of who invented it, but it was called to my attention by my friend Wally Wilson. I have added a minor touch.

You'll need three coins: a dime, a quarter, and a half-dollar. In presentation, you can probably borrow a dime and a quarter, but not too many people carry a half-dollar. So when you plan to perform the trick, you should probably have a half-dollar available. (In the *Notes* at the end, I'll explain how you can perform the trick without using American coins.)

Ask Janet to assist you. Place the three coins onto the table, saying, "Janet, we're going to use these in a moment to test your psychic ability. Sometimes an astonishing coincidence occurs, and, of course, sometimes it doesn't."

Go through the deck and find a 2. Place this face up onto the table. On top of it place another 2 of any other suit. On top of this place a pair of face-up 4's of any suits. These are followed by pairs of 6's, 8's, 10's, and Q's. There are six pairs in all. From the face down, here is the layout:

Q Q 10 10 8 8 6 6 4 4 2 2

Make no attempt to hide the fact that each pair consists of matching values, but don't call attention to it either. Actually, the six pairs could be of any different values; this method, raising the value by two each time, guarantees that you won't accidentally have two pairs of the same value.

Set the rest of the deck aside. Pick up the pile of pairs, saying, "I'd better mix them up a bit."

You now perform an up-and-down shuffle. (See *The Up-and-Down Shuffle*, page 11.) In the first move, your right hand takes the top card and moves forward a few inches. The next card goes below the first one and extends *toward* you. Continue alternating like this through the packet. Strip out the lower group and set these cards on top of those remaining in your left hand. Set the packet onto the table. Turn it face down.

"Janet, please give the cards a cut. And you may cut the cards as many more times as you wish."

Her complete cuts do not change the basic order. So the up-and-down shuffle has arranged the cards so that the top six cards are in the same order as the bottom six. (Be sure to perform the up-and-down shuffle *before* the packet is cut; otherwise, this vital setup could be ruined.)

The cards now might look like this, from the face to the top:

6 8 10 Q 2 4 6 8 10 Q 2 4

The cards could actually be set up like this at the beginning, but I prefer my method, which creates the illusion that the cards are thoroughly mixed.

At this point, you might ask another spectator to give the packet a cut or two.

Pick up the packet and do the following:

(1) Deal a face-down row of three cards, going from left to right.

(2) Below that, deal another face-down row of three cards, again going from left to right.

(3) Deal one face-down card on top of each card in that second row, going from left to right.

(4) Repeat (3). (See Illus. 23 for the present position, from your point of view.)

Say to Janet, "Please pick up the three coins and distribute them so that one is on top of each one of these cards." Indicate the first row of cards you dealt.

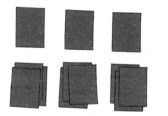

Illus. 23

Note the coin that rests on the card on your left. Let's say that it's the quarter. Call Janet's attention to it. Pick up the three-card pile on your left. "Janet, you placed the quarter on the card above this pile. I'll spell the word *quarter*, moving one card from the top to the bottom of this pile for each letter." Do so. Then take the card which is now on top of the pile and place it on top of the coin whose name you just spelled. The quarter now rests on a card and has another card on top of it. "As you can see, Janet, we now have a sort of coin sandwich."

You pick up the middle pile of three cards and, in the same

way as above, spell out the name of the coin above it. Place the top card of this pile on top of the coin you just spelled.

Do the same with the last pile.

"Don't forget, Janet: You cut the cards a number of times, and you had complete freedom of choice as to where to put the coins. Now let's see how you did."

Turn the two cards over that surround the first coin. The cards are of the same value. Do the same with the cards that surround the second coin. And, of course, repeat with the cards that surround the third coin.

For most, this will seem an excellent trick, so pause a moment to let it sink in. Then: "I thought that was an amazing coincidence, Janet, but I can see that you're not too impressed. Let's see if there are any more coincidences."

Turn each of the remaining pairs face up. That is, turn over each pair that remains in the second row. Each pair consists of two cards of the same value.

"Now *there's* a coincidence!"

Notes

(1) Why does the trick work? When you spell out the value of the coin in your three-card pile, you want to end up with the top card being the original second card from the top. This will happen when the spelling consists of four letters (dime), seven letters (quarter), or ten letters (half-dollar). Obviously, you just keep adding three, so the spelling would work out with words consisting of 13 letters, 16, 19, 22, etc. It's amazingly ingenious, I believe, that the inventor took advantage of the various spellings to fashion this astounding trick.

(2) You can readily work the trick without using American coins. You must find small objects which spell out with four letters, seven letters, and ten letters respectively.

The theme could be snacks, for instance. Four-letter objects could be *soda or cola* (a can); seven-letter ones could be *pretzel, popcorn,* or *cracker*; and a ten-letter one could be *potato chip.*

Many possibilities are available when you use no particular theme. Four-letter objects could be *ring, comb, book,* or *fork*; seven-letter objects could be *key ring* or *glasses*; ten-letter objects could be *spectacles, wristwatch,* or *tiny bottle.*

Undoubtedly, many other possibilities will occur to you.

GOOD LUCK

Ron Bauer is one of magic's truly great innovators. He is also among the leaders of those who have had their tricks "borrowed" without credit. In fact, some of the best known names in magic have reinvented some of Ron's tricks.

Ron revised a trick by Johann Hofsinzer, famous 19th-century magician, eliminating all sleight of hand. He then gave me permission to use it in this book. I've added a minor touch to the ending.

Required is a small setup. Make the setup by placing any ace face up on the table. On top of it place a face-up 2, then a 3, and then a 4. Continue on through 10. Place this stack face down on top of the deck. Put another card on top. So this is your setup from the top of the deck down:

x (any card) A 2 3 4 5 6 7 8 9 10

Set the deck down in front of Marge and turn away. "Marge, please think of a number from 1 to 10. Now pick up the deck and deal that many cards into a pile. When you finish, set the deck down on the table." When she finishes, continue: "Now pick up the pile you counted off and hide those cards somewhere."

Turn back to the group. Pick up the deck, saying, "Marge, I'd like you to choose a card." You now perform *The Double-Turnover Force*, as described on page 12.

At the end, you fan through the face-up cards to the first face-down card. Hold the face-up cards, still fanned out, in your right hand. Thumb off the first face-down card onto the table, saying, "There's your card."

Set the cards in your right hand down. Spread them out with your right hand. "You have a great many cards here that you could have chosen." Turn the cards in your left hand face up and casually fan them out so that all can see them. But don't fan them all the way to the top; you don't want to reveal what's left of your setup. Drop the cards you're holding on top of the face-up cards on the table. Gather the cards up, turn them face down, and set them aside.

"Marge, please take the cards from where you've hidden them." Hold your hand out to take the packet. Count them onto the table one at a time. Let's say the number is 5. "I count 5. Is that what you took?" She says yes.

"Good." Drop the cards on top of the deck. Pick up the deck and give it a casual shuffle as you proceed with your patter.

"Marge, once in a while, when trying this experiment, I'll run into a coincidence, or perhaps some mysterious relationship between the spectator and the cards." Tap the "chosen" card. "If that were to operate here, this card would be the same as the number of cards in your packet. The packet had five cards in it. Let's look at the card you picked." Turn over the card. "A five. Marvelous! How did you do it?"

Note

At the beginning of the trick, you're instructed to set the deck in front of Marge and then turn away. Why don't you simply hand her the deck? Experience tells me that if you hand out the deck too soon, the spectator might automatically start shuffling. Clearly, with this trick that would be a disaster.

REVERSE TRICKS

JEALOUSY

How about something old and something new? The plot is old, and my handling is new.

Hand the deck to Matt and ask him to give it a good shuffle. You take the cards back and turn over the top card. "I can't believe what you've done, Matt." Suppose the card is the 3C. "You've shuffled to the top the most jealous card in the deck, the three of clubs. You did a good job, because the three of clubs really likes being on top."

Turn the 3C face down, but in a particular way. Push it off the deck with your left thumb; then grasp it on the outer right corner with the right hand, thumb on top, fingers below (Illus. 24). Turn the card end-for-end, replacing it on the deck face down. This whole procedure enables you to get a little-finger break below the 3C as you put it back onto the deck. (See *When Putting Cards on Top of the Deck,* page 9.)

Illus. 24

You now perform a sleight known as the Braue Reversal, named after its inventor, Fred Braue. You're holding the deck in the dealing position in your left hand. Take over the break with your right thumb. (See *Transferring the Break to the Right Thumb*, page 9.) You're now primarily holding the deck with the right hand. With the palm-up left hand, take the bottom half of the deck and move it to the left (Illus. 25). Stick your left thumb beneath this packet. Now it's quite easy to flip the packet over, using your left thumb. Place the packet on top of the deck, lifting your right first finger to allow passage. *Continue holding the break with your right thumb.* Naturally, a card is now on view on top of the deck. It's the original bottom card of those you turned over. Let's suppose that it's the AH. "The ace of hearts is not a jealous card...not like the three of clubs."

Illus. 25

With the left hand, take all the cards *below the break you are holding with your right thumb,* flip these over with your left thumb, and place them face up on top. Another card is now on view at the top of the deck. Let's say that it's the JS. "And the jack of spades doesn't have a jealous bone in his body. No, Matt. The three of clubs is the jealous one."

You're now holding a face-up deck, except for the lowermost card—the face-down 3C.

"And do you know who he's most jealous of? His brother, the three of spades. I'll show you what I mean."

Fan through the face-up cards and find the 3S, take it out, and place it on top of the card on the face of the deck. As you do this, make sure you don't inadvertently show the back of the 3C, which is at the back of the face-up deck.

"Let me demonstrate. "I'm going to treat the 3S in a very special way—so that he'll be faced differently from all the other cards." Lift off the 3S, turn it over, and push it into the deck about a quarter of the way down.

Cut off about half the cards and place them beneath the other half. Turn the deck face down.

"Do you think the three of clubs can stand that? Oh, no, he's extremely jealous." Fan down to the face-up 3S and pull it out of the deck partway. "See, here's the three of spades."

Continue fanning to the 3C and pull it partway from the deck. "And here's his jealous brother. He just *had* to face the same way."

Pause.

"Thank goodness *people* aren't like that."

Note

At the end of the trick, the face-down cards are spread out somewhat and the two matching face-up cards are sticking out nearly half their length (Illus. 26). This makes quite a striking display; give spectators a chance to see it and enjoy it.

Illus. 26

THREE IN ONE

Here again is an old basic principle, to which I've added a new idea, along with unusual handling and a convincing touch. What I like most about this trick is that so much is accomplished with so little effort.

The only preparation is to get two aces on the bottom of the deck. This can usually be done between tricks while chatting with the group. If at all possible, the aces should be of the same color.

Melissa plays cards quite often, so hold the deck out to her, saying, "Melissa, please cut off a small packet of cards. Then look through your packet and take out any card you wish. Set the rest of your packet aside."

Without explanation, you turn away. While she follows your instructions, secretly take the ace from the bottom of your packet, turn it over, and place it on top. Turn over the other ace that's on the bottom and leave it face up on the bottom. Turn the entire packet over. The entire packet is now face up except for a face-down ace on top and another on the bottom. It appears, however, that you're holding a face-down packet.

Turn back to the group. "Concentrate on your card, Melissa." Pause for a few seconds. "I can't seem to get it. Let's try something else. Please turn your card face up and set it onto the table." Suppose the card is the jack of hearts. You want to be sure everyone remembers it, so you say, "Oh, yes, the jack of hearts. I knew it was a face card." Or make a similar comment, naming the card.

Drop your packet on top of the face-up card, saying, "Let's get your card face up on the bottom of the deck."

Pick up the packet with your palm-down right hand, thumb at the left inner end and fingers at the outer end (Illus. 27). Casually turn your hand over and back, showing that a face-down card is at each end. "But first, Melissa, would you please count the rest of the cards that you cut off. If the number is odd, we'll know absolutely that this experiment will work."

As she counts the cards, you transfer the cards to the left hand and, in the process, subtly turn the packet over. Here's

Illus. 27

how. You're still holding the packet in the grip shown in Illus. 27. Tilt the right hand clockwise so that the sides of the packet are perpendicular to the floor. Take the packet into the left hand as though you're about to perform an overhand shuffle (Illus. 28). Turn the left hand clockwise. The packet is now turned over (Illus. 29). No one will notice. There are a number of reasons: (1) The handling is subtle. (2) No one has any reason to watch closely, for no one has any idea of what you intend to do. (3) The misdirection is enormous.

Illus. 28

Illus. 29

When Melissa finishes her count, ask her, "Is the number odd or even?" If she says that it's odd, express your satisfaction. If not, say, "Oh-oh! I may be in trouble."

With your right hand, adjust your packet so that the left hand is holding it in the dealing position. With the right hand, cut off about half the packet and set it face down onto the table. Take the other half into the palm-down right hand. Turn the hand over, showing the back of the bottom card. "Your card," you comment. Retaining this position, with the tips of the left fingers draw the bottom card to the left, revealing the card below it (Illus. 30). Make no comment; just return the bottom card to its original position.

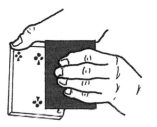

Illus. 30

Now place this packet on top of the packet on the table. "So there's your card, face up in the middle of the packet." Casually glance at the cards that Melissa counted. "We'd better have all the cards." Pick up the counted cards and place them on top of your packet.

"I'm going to attempt three astonishing feats. First, I'm going to try to turn your card over so that it becomes face down." Tap the top of the deck a few times. "There. I think that should do it."

Pause. "Say, does anyone here play poker?" Surely someone does. "Tell me, what would be a pretty good pair to hold."

Chances are someone will say, "A pair of aces."

If not, say, "That's good, all right, but I'd prefer aces." In either instance, continue, "Let's see if I can turn two aces so that they're face up." Tap the top of the deck several times. "I hope that worked." Pause. "This is exhausting."

"Let's see if it worked."

Fan through the face-down cards. "We're looking for two face-up aces, and we want to see if your chosen card is face down. Ah, there are the aces. And there's a face-down card between them."

Remove in a group the two face-up aces along with the face-down card between them. Set the rest of the deck aside.

Remove the face-down card between the aces. "And what was your card, Melissa?" She names it, and you turn over the one you're holding.

WOULD I LIE?

I contrived the following stunt to fool magicians. As luck would have it, it works well with lay audiences as well.

Announce to the group, "I'll teach you how magicians try to fool you."

Have Alex take a card, look at it, show it around, and return it to the deck. You keep the cards fanned so that Alex can still see where his card is.

"So you've returned your card to the deck, Alex. Now I'll do this slowly so that you can see exactly what happens."

The cards are still fanned and Alex can clearly see his card's location. With your right hand, pick up all the cards above the selected one. Lift your left hand and, with your left thumb, push off the top card of the group it's holding, letting all get a look at the chosen card. Lower your left hand and pull the card back on top.

Turn the cards in your right hand face up and set them evenly on top of the face-down group in your left hand.

"The magician will say, 'You had your choice of all these cards.'" Fan through the face-up cards. When you come to the face-down cards, fan out at least two extra cards and then stop (Illus. 31). Keeping your right hand palm up, close up the face-up cards, adding the chosen card to the bottom.

Illus. 31

With the face-up cards in your right hand, tap the top card of the face-down cards in your left hand. As you tap the middle of the card, give a little wink. Put your left thumb under the cards in your left hand and flip the cards over so that they're face up. All the cards are now face up. Rest the packet in your right hand on the right edge of the packet in your left hand. With the left thumb, fan through the cards in your left hand, showing their faces, but stop several cards short of the top.

"The magician will say, 'Or you could have chosen any one of these.' But of course he doesn't fan through all the way. And he'll say, 'So you had all these cards to choose from.'"

Close up the deck and turn it face down.

"So where's the chosen card? Right. On top. In position for the magician to do any trick he wants to. For example, he could stick it into the middle of the deck, like this." Take off the top card and slide it into the middle of the deck. Tap the deck. "Then he could bring the card back to the top." Turn over the top card. "Right?"

Alex will deny that you've turned his card over.

Look mildly peeved. "Of course that isn't your card. I didn't say that *I* was going to do that; I said that some magicians would do that. If *I* were going to do something magical, I'd do this." With your knuckles, knock the top of the deck a few times. "What's the name of your card?"

Alex names it. You fan down through the cards and show him that his card is now face up in the middle of the deck.

FOUR-ACE TRICKS

WHERE ARE THE ACES?

Decades ago, I wrote a booklet called *The Invisible Deck and Other Card Tricks*, which was published by the Ireland Magic Co. Included in the booklet was my original trick, "Where Are the Aces?" Unfortunately, perhaps, I don't recall seeing anyone perform this trick except me. Maybe you'll like it; it has a lovely surprise ending.

The only preparation is to have the two red aces on top of the deck. Go through the deck, find the black aces, and toss them face up onto the table. Since Kate is usually very attentive, she'd be the ideal assistant.

"Kate, I'd like you to watch very carefully. I'm going to see if you can see what happens to the aces."

Place one black ace on top of the deck and the other on the bottom of the deck. Hold the deck from above in the left hand, fingers at the far end and thumb at the near end. With the right hand, draw off the top and bottom cards together. (See *Milking the Cards*, page 12.)

Place these two cards together on top of the deck. Draw off two more cards in the same way; again, these two are placed together on top of the deck. Once more, milk two cards from the deck; these two are placed together *on the bottom*. So, three times you draw off two cards. The first two times, they are placed on top; the third time, they are placed on the bottom.

The next move can be difficult for some. If you find it so, you may prefer doing a substitute move which I describe in a note at the end of the trick. Grip the deck in the left hand, thumb on top and fingers on the bottom. A few inches away, and parallel to the left hand, is the palm-up right hand (Illus.

32). Keep a light pressure on the top and bottom cards as you make a tossing motion toward your right hand. The top and bottom cards are retained in the left hand; the rest of the deck lands in the right hand (Illus. 33).

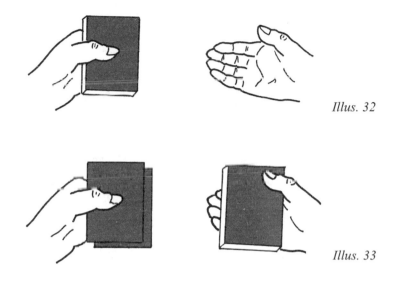

Illus. 32

Illus. 33

The right hand now grips the deck as the left hand had— thumb on top and fingers on the bottom. The right hand retains the top and bottom cards while tossing the remainder of the deck to the left, so that it lands on the table.

You're now holding two cards in each hand, the black aces in the right hand and two indifferent cards in the left.

"Kate, have you been watching carefully? Good. Point to the hand that holds the aces."

If Kate chooses the black aces, show them, and congratulate her. Also, show the cards in the other hand. If she chooses the wrong hand, show the cards in both hands, and assure Kate that she'll get another chance.

Place the indifferent cards on the bottom of the deck. As before, one black ace goes on top and the other on the bottom.

"Keep your eyes open now, Kate."

Milk two cards and place them on top of the deck. Again milk two cards and place them on the bottom of the deck. Finally, milk two cards and place them on top of the deck.

Once more toss the deck into the right hand, retaining the top and bottom cards in the left hand. Toss the deck onto the table, retaining the top and bottom cards in the right hand.

"Are you ready, Kate? Point to the hand that holds the aces."

When she points, proceed exactly as before. The four cards are shown. The indifferent cards are placed on the bottom. Then one black ace goes on top, the other on the bottom.

"This time we'll make it even easier for you, Kate. Let's see if you can figure out which hand *doesn't* hold the aces."

Milk two cards and place them on the bottom. Again milk two cards and place them on the bottom. Finally milk two cards and place them on top. Follow the usual tossing procedure, ending up with two cards in each hand.

"Okay, Kate, point to the hand that *doesn't* hold the aces."

She points to one hand. If she points to the left hand, show her the red aces in that hand. Also, display the black aces in the right hand. "Sorry, Kate. You didn't have a chance."

If Kate points to the right hand, show the black aces. *Don't show the red aces that are in the left hand.* Instead, simply return them to the *top* of the deck. As usual, one black ace goes on top of the deck, the other to the bottom of the deck. You then repeat the procedure just described.

If Kate insists on missing again, you might repeat the stunt again. This time, however, it's probably best to "accidentally" give her a peek at the two black aces before she chooses. No use going on forever.

Twice the spectator guesses where the aces are. The third time she guesses where the aces aren't. Here's a handy way to remember how you place the milked cards each time: (1) Top-top-bottom. (2) Top-bottom-top. (3) Bottom-bottom-top.

Note

If you have trouble tossing the deck while retaining the top and bottom cards, you might try this much easier procedure: Milk two cards as described above. Set these cards down to the right. Milk two more cards and set them down to the left. Ask the spectator to point to the pair that she thinks are the aces.

A GOOD CUT OF CHUCK

I don't know who originated this trick, but it was shown to me by Chuck Golay, who I'm sure added touches of his own. It's that rare trick which requires little skill but gives the impression of incredible dexterity.

Fan through the deck, saying, "I'll need the four aces." When you come to a 5, cut the cards so that it becomes second from the top of the deck. "They have to be here somewhere." Toss the aces face up onto the table as you come to them.

Arrange the aces in a face-up row. Turn the deck face down. Cut from the top about a quarter of the cards and place the face-down packet below the ace on the left. (The packet is placed nearer to you.) Cut from the top about a third of the remaining cards and place the packet below the second ace from the right. Cut off about half of the remaining cards and place this packet below the second ace from the left. Place the remaining cards below the ace on the right. In other words, about a quarter of the deck is below each ace, with the original top portion of the deck being the pile on the left.

Pick up the packet on the left. (As you recall, the second card from the top of this packet is a 5.) Turn the packet face up and fan through the cards so that you can see which card is sixth from the original top. Pick up the ace on the left and place it to the right of this card. So the first ace is now seventh from the original top of the packet you're holding in your left hand (Illus. 34). Close up the packet.

With your right hand, pick up the packet which is now on the left. Turn it face up and place it on top of the cards in your

Illus. 34

left hand. Pick up the ace on the left and place it on top of the cards in your left hand.

Fan back through the cards, showing how widely the two aces are separated. When you fan back to the face of the packet, get a break with the tip of your left little finger under the fourth card from the face. (See *Below a Small Number from the Top*, page 9.) Give the cards a double-cut, cutting the three cards above the break to the back of the face-up group. (See *Double-Cut*, page 10.)

Pick up the present packet on the left, turn it face up, and put it on top of the face-up cards in your left hand. Reach with your right hand to pick up the ace now on the left. As you do so, secure a break under the top card with your left little finger. (See *Below the Top Card*, page 9.) The action of reaching for the ace provides plenty of misdirection. Pick up the ace and place it face up on top of the packet. You're now holding a little-finger break beneath the top two cards of the packet. In a double-cut, move these two cards to the back of the face-up packet.

Handle the last packet and ace in exactly the same way as you did the third packet and ace.

The cards from the top are now in this order, x standing for any card:

x A x A x x x A x 5 x x x x A

Even up the cards and hold them up so that all can see that no cards are sticking out and that you're holding no breaks. *But don't say anything to that effect!*

Turn the deck face down.

"Let's see if I can find any of the aces."

Lift the deck with your right hand. Turn your hand over, showing that the bottom card of the deck is not an ace. Place the deck face down into your left hand. Push off the top card with your left thumb. Take this card with your palm-down right hand, thumb at the inner end, fingers at the outer end. Lift it and show its face (Illus. 35). As you return the card to the top of the deck, you easily hold a break with your right thumb between the card and the rest of the deck. Your right fingers are holding the outer end of the deck, while the right thumb holds the break along with the inner end of the deck.

Illus. 35

You're now going to perform a triple-cut, which is a variation of *The Double-Cut*, on page 10. The left hand takes about *a third* of the cards from the bottom and places them on top, still retaining the break held by your right thumb. Again with the left hand, move a third of the cards from the bottom to the top. Now the left hand takes the remainder of the cards below the break and puts them on top. The upshot is that the top card which you showed is now on the bottom, and an ace is on top of the deck.

Turn the ace over, showing it, and place it face up onto the table.

To get a second ace, repeat all these moves. Finally, show the ace on top and place it onto the table next to the first ace.

Turn the deck face up and fan out several cards at the bottom, showing that there's no ace there. Turn the deck face down. Fan

Illus. 36

out three cards from the top. Take them in your right hand. Hold your hand up, displaying the faces (Illus. 36). As you replace them face down on top, get a break beneath them with the tip of your left little finger.

Once more you perform the triple-cut, bringing these three cards to the bottom. On top is an ace, which you turn over and deal onto the table next to the other two.

Lastly, you repeat the moves you used for the first two aces. This time, when you turn over the top card, it turns out to be a 5. "A five!" you declare, clearly disappointed. "We might as well use it."

Set the 5 aside face up. Slowly deal five cards from the top into a pile on the table, counting aloud. Turn over the last card dealt. It's the final ace.

"Thank goodness," you declare, placing the final ace next to the other three.

A CUT ABOVE THE REST

Once more the aces are cut, but this time by a *spectator*. This is probably the easiest and most direct of all tricks in which the aces are cut. The only problem is that a sneaky sleight is required. Very few can do the sleight undetectably, so most performers require considerable misdirection. Far better, I figure, to use an easier version of the sleight.

To begin the trick, you must have two aces on top of the deck and two on the bottom. This is easily accomplished in one of two ways: You can start with this trick. Or you can do a four-ace trick earlier in your performance and keep the aces together during ensuing tricks. All you need do, then, is fan through the cards, faces toward yourself, and cut between the aces, bringing two to the bottom and two to the top.

Single out Evelyn. "You look pretty magical to me, Evelyn. How about helping me out."

As you're saying this, you perform the easy sleight I mentioned above.

Turn clockwise about 45 degrees, so that your left side is mostly toward the group. With the left hand, hold the deck of cards in a variation of the dealing position: The thumb is along the left side of the deck instead of on top, and your left hand is tilted clockwise so that the sides of the deck are parallel to the floor (Illus. 37).

Illus. 37

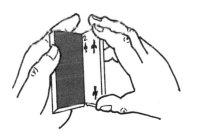

Illus. 38

You grip a small group of cards at the top of the deck—ten or so—with your right thumb at the inner end and fingers at the outer end. The grip should be taken on the left side of the cards. You now move the top side of these cards away from the rest of the deck by pivoting the group sideways to the right, as though starting to open the back of a book (Illus. 38).

Your left fingers press against the back of these cards as you pull them up and away from the rest of the deck. The small group clears, but its top card stays as it is pressed against the top of the remaining deck (Illus. 39).

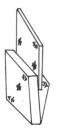

Illus. 39

You let the main deck fall so that it is face down in the dealing position in the left hand. Meanwhile, your right hand holds up the small pile you have apparently cut from the top.

(If you choose to do no sleight at all, I have provided a method in the notes at the end.)

The situation: The main deck is face down in your left hand with an ace on top, which you drew from the top of the small packet in your right hand. There are two more aces on the bottom of the main deck. And there is one more ace on top of the small packet you hold in your right hand.

Let everyone see the size of the packet you're holding in your right hand. "See this packet, Evelyn? I'd like you to cut off a small packet also. It can be a little smaller or a little larger. But don't make it too large, because you're going to have to make three more cuts."

Hold out your left hand so that Evelyn can cut a packet from the main deck. After she takes a packet, have her place it face down onto the table. Compliment her on the quality of her cut. "I don't believe anyone could have cut off a packet any more efficiently than you did, Evelyn."

Meanwhile, you casually place your small packet on top of the cards in your left hand.

"Try it again, Evelyn." Hold out the cards so that she can cut off another packet. This one is also placed face down onto the table.

Two packets are face down on the table, each having an ace on top. There are two aces on the bottom of the deck.

As you compliment Evelyn this time, perform an overhand shuffle. With the first move, you squeeze your left fingers and thumb together, drawing off the top and bottom cards together. In a continuous motion, shuffle off the rest of the cards. When you near the last of the cards, shuffle them singly. The result of the shuffle is that the second card from the bottom (an ace) is on top of the deck and that the bottom card of the deck is still an ace.

Offer the deck for Evelyn to cut off another packet, which she sets face down onto the table. While lavishly praising her technique, you give the deck another overhand shuffle. Again when you near the last few cards, you shuffle them singly, thus bringing the bottom card (an ace) to the top.

Evelyn cuts off a final packet and places it face down onto the table.

"Evelyn, it's truly wonderful the way you've cut off such perfect small packets. I don't think I've ever seen anyone do that quite so well before. It's almost as though you're a professional. Let's see how you did."

Turn over the top card of each packet. Evelyn has succeeded in cutting the four aces!

"I don't know about the rest of you, but I don't think I'll *ever* play cards with Evelyn."

Note

The easy sleight described above is completely hidden. If, however, you feel sheepish about it, you can perform it while strolling about, chatting. In effect, you perform the move before anyone has reason to believe you're even going to perform a trick.

Another possibility is this: Perform *The Double-Turnover Force*, on page 12. You have just fanned through the face-up cards to the first face-down card. A small group of face-up cards is in your right hand. Set these *face down* onto the table.

"Your card," you say, picking up the top card of those in your left hand and placing it face down on top of the pile on the table.

The spectator has cut her first ace. You have an ace on top of the deck and two aces on the bottom, and can now proceed.

COLLECTIBLES

The basic trick here has to be one of the first four-ace tricks ever invented. This handling, however, makes it more interesting, I believe, and totally deceptive.

The four aces are face up on the table. "I would like to perform two tricks for you; one is really excellent, and the other is just so-so."

Regine was always an eager volunteer in high school, so ask her to assist you. "Regine, I'm going to turn my back, and, while my back is turned, I'd like you to pick out one of the aces and turn it face down."

She just might protest that this is really a stupid idea. Pay no attention; in fact, talk over her, repeating that all she need do is turn one of the aces face down.

While your back is turned, cut off the upper half of the deck and turn the lower half over. Replace the upper half of the deck. Half the deck is now facing the other half. Grip the deck in the left hand in the dealing position.

Turn back to the group. Take a quick glance at the aces, noting which one is missing. Let's say that it's the AH. Avert your head quickly, acting as though you hadn't looked. "Concentrate on the ace you turned over, Regine. I'd say it's the ace of hearts."

Undoubtedly many will declare that your trick is quite silly.

Own up to it. "You're right, you're right. That wasn't very good." As you speak, gather up the other three aces and put them face down on top of the deck, which is still in the dealing position in your left hand. Let your left hand drop to your side.

"You know what the real problem is? *That* was the really excellent trick."

As you say this, bring your left hand up, *palm down* (Illus. 40). You have turned the deck over. Take it by the far end into your right hand, thumb on top, fingers on the bottom (Illus. 41). Make some innocuous remark, such as, "Well, that's the way it goes."

Illus. 40

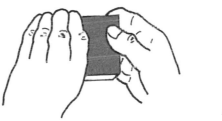

Illus. 41

As you make the remark, place the deck in the left hand in the dealing position. The aces are now face up on the bottom of the deck, followed by a number of other face-up cards. Deal the top three cards face down into a row, mumbling, "Let's see…we'll put the aces here. And we'd better put some cards on top of them."

Fan off about six cards from the top of the deck and place

them face down on top of the presumed ace on the left. In the same way, put about five cards on top of the middle card. And put about four cards onto the card on the right.

Your left hand is holding the remainder of the deck. Again, let this hand drop to your side. As you do this, say to Regine, "Please turn over the ace you selected." Point to the face-down ace with your right hand. She turns the ace face up.

You are about the turn the deck over again. As described above, bring the deck up, take it in your right hand, and place it in the dealing position back into your left hand.

Fan off three cards from the top and place these face down on top of the face-up ace. These, of course, are the other three aces.

Still holding the deck in your left hand, turn over the three piles one by one, showing that the aces are not there. As you turn them over, pile one face up on top of the other. Set the packet that is in your left hand on top of all. (The face cards on the bottom of the packet blend in with the other face-up cards, leaving you "clean.")

"Good heavens! What became of the aces?"

Turn over the three face-down aces, leaving all four aces displayed face up on the table.

While everyone is gasping and nominating you for high office, fan through the cards on the table. Turn all the face-down cards over so that the entire packet is face up. Pick up the packet and give it a little shuffle.

FOUR FOR ACES

Les Nixon is responsible for the first mention I've found of this startling puzzler.

You ask four spectators to help out. Explain to them, "We're about to conduct a scientific experiment. We'll try to find out if you four have *anything* in common. First, I'll give each of you an ace and five other cards."

Do so. "I'd like you all to shuffle your six cards. Mix them up really well."

When they finish, continue: "Please, each of you fan your cards out so that only you can see their faces. Notice what number your ace is from the top. Please remember that number. Now turn your cards face down. Move three cards from the top to the bottom of your pile." Pause. "Remember that number that I asked you to remember? Please move that number from the top to the bottom of your pile." Pause. "Just for good measure, move one more card from the top to the bottom."

Address just one spectator: "Please gather up the piles in any order you wish." As he gathers the piles one on top of the other in any order, make sure he does not misconstrue your instructions to include shuffling. Take the cards from the spectator.

"Continuing the experiment, we'll need six piles." Deal the cards into six piles as though dealing six hands of cards. The second pile is critical, for it consists of all four aces. You are about to force the selection of this pile through a so-called "magician's choice."

"We'll need to make some choices here." Ask Buster, one of your assistants, to help out

Spread your right hand out and place it on the table so that it touches the three piles on the right. Put your left hand on the table so that it touches the three piles on the left.

Address Buster, "What'll it be, right or left?"

Whatever he replies, gather up the three piles on *your* right and set them aside.

Turn to Maxine. Gesture toward the three remaining piles. "Please hand me a pile, Maxine."

If she hands you the pile containing the aces, fine. Say, "I think it's quite obvious that you four have a psychic bond." Deal the aces face up one at a time.

Otherwise, set the pile aside with the other three you discarded.

It's Pam's turn. "Pam, I'd like you to pick a pile."

She will either pick up one of the two remaining piles, or

she will point to one. If she chooses the one containing the aces, discard the other, saying, "Excellent choice, Pam." Proceed to the end as described above.

If she chooses the other, discard it. Point to the remaining pile, saying, "And that leaves us with this pile" Pick it up and proceed to the end.

Review

(1) Four spectators are each given six cards, including an ace.

(2) They are given these instructions:

    A. Mix your cards.

    B. Fan them out so that only you can see the faces and note what number your ace is from the top. Remember that number.

    C. Turn your cards face down. Move three cards from the top to the bottom of your pile.

    D. Recall the number you were to remember? Move that number from the top to the bottom of your pile.

    E. For good measure, move one more card from the top to the bottom of your pile.

(3) One spectator gathers up the piles in any order.

(4) You deal the cards into six piles. Through "magician's choice," you force the selection of pile 2, which contains all four aces.

Notes

(1) If you wished, you could have the spectators do all the moves. But with this trick, I like to handle the cards, thus offering the possibility that the trick is not totally automatic.

(2) Why does this trick work? If we change the order of the instructions, I think the answer will be apparent.

The spectator has noted the number of his ace from the top of his packet. Suppose your instructions follow this order:

(A) Remember that number I asked you to remember. Please move that number from the top to the bottom of your pile. (Where is the ace? On the bottom of the pile.)

(B) Move three cards from the top to the bottom of your pile. (Where is the ace? Third card from the top.)

(C) Just for good measure, move one more card from the top to the bottom. (The ace is now second from the top.)

SPELLING TRICKS

MAGIC LOCATOR

Al Smith developed an excellent variation of a well-known principle. The trick has amazing impact when you consider the simplicity of method.

Approach Rob as you fan through the face-down cards. "Just touch a card, please, Rob." When he does so, turn the card face up in place. Name the card. Suppose it's the 7S. "All right, Rob, you chose the seven of spades." Fan through several more cards and get a break with the tip of your left little finger beneath the third card below the face-up card. (This is the same move involved in *When a Card Is Returned*, page 8.) As you do this, say, "You might have touched any one of these cards. Or, in fact, any other card in the deck." This latter statement you make as you close up the cards.

In our example, you'd now have a face-up seven of spades, followed by three cards and your inserted little finger.

Casually double-cut the cards so that the face-up card becomes fourth from the bottom. (See *The Double Cut*, on page 10.)

Hand the deck to Rob. "Deal the cards into a pile, Rob." After he has dealt several cards, say, "You can stop whenever you wish."

He stops. "Please look at the last card dealt and show it around."

When he's done showing it around, continue, "Put it back on top of your pile, and put the rest of the deck on top of it. Finally, give the deck a complete cut."

You talk to the group for a bit, both to build up the trick and to help the spectators forget precisely what has happened. So you might say, "I had no way of knowing what card you'd elect to have turned over. And I could not have guessed what card you'd choose. But I think there might be a close relationship between the two cards. Let's find out."

Holding the cards down so that all can see, you fan through the face-down deck to the face-up card. Leave the face-up card on top of those in your left hand. Set the rest of the deck aside.

"Let's see if we can spell out the value of this card to find the one you chose."

All the values will spell out with either three, four, or five letters.

Let's say that the value of the face-up card spells out with three letters (ace, two, six, ten). Set aside the face-up card. Pick up the deck and spell out the value of the card, dealing one card onto the table for each letter. Turn over the next card.

If the value spells out with four letters (four, five, nine, jack, king), set aside the face-up card. Pick up the deck and spell out the value, turning over the last card dealt.

If the value spells out with five letters (three, seven, eight, queen), pick up the deck, *leaving the face-up card on top*. Spell out the value of the card, turning over the last card dealt.

In each instance, ask for the name of the chosen card before turning it over.

A NAME TO CONJURE WITH

Stewart James adapted an excellent principle in creating one of the easiest of all spelling tricks.

First, you must know the name of the spectator you're going to work with. To start the trick, then, you fan through the cards and give your assistant a stack. How many cards? Twice the number of letters in his name, plus one card. Suppose his name is John Smith. Clearly, his name consists of 9 letters. You double that, getting 18, and then you add 1 more, for a total of 19. So John Smith would receive 19 cards.

You don't want to appear to be counting them, however. So it's best to fan through three cards at a time. "Here," you say, "let me give you a good-sized pile of cards." Hand the stack to him and set the rest of the deck onto the table. "Please shuffle them, John."

Turn your back. "Think of a small number, say from one to five. Count off that number from your packet to the top of the deck." Pause. "Now count down to that same number in your pile and look at the card that lies at that number. Remember that card. Even up the packet."

Turn back and take the packet. Give it a false cut, if you can. If you can't, put the packet behind your back, saying, "I'm going to move some cards around. There!" Riffle the ends of the packet a few times and then bring the packet forward.

"Here's what I'd like you to do, John. Spell out your name, like this." Spell out his name, transferring one card from the top to the bottom for each letter. Hand him the packet. He does the same. When he's done, have him turn over the present top card. It's the one he chose.

MAGIC IS MY BUSINESS

The basic principle used in this trick was developed, I believe, by Alex Elmsley. As far as I know, my use of the principle is unique. This is one of those rare puzzlers in which the deck is never handled by the magician.

Hand Beatrice the deck and turn your back.

Provide these instructions, with appropriate pauses: "Please shuffle the deck, Beatrice. Now just *think* of any card. Fan through the deck and find that card. Remove it from the deck and place it face up onto the table."

When she's ready, continue: "Let's say that you're to spell out the name of a card, using one card for each letter in the spelling. No one could possibly know how many cards are on the table. After all, the queen of diamonds has many more letters than, say, the two of clubs. So please pick up the deck and spell out the name of your card, dealing one card into a pile for each letter in the name."

Give her a chance to finish, then: "When you're done, put the rest of the deck aside. We're only going to use the cards you spelled out onto the table and your chosen card. So please turn your chosen card face down and place it on top of those you spelled out onto the table."

Turn back and face Beatrice, assuming, of course, that she hasn't absconded with your brand-new deck of cards.

"In a moment, Beatrice, I'll want you to spell out a sentence. You'll spell out, 'Magic is my business.' Now if you prefer, you can spell out, 'My business is magic.' Or you can spell out 'My magic is business.' Or perhaps, 'Business is *my* magic.' Or maybe you'd prefer a philosophical sentence, like, 'Is magic my business?' Or even, 'Is business my magic?' Or you can even make an exclamation, like, 'My! business *is* magic.' You have complete freedom of choice...any one of these sentences."

She chooses one of these—or any other 17-letter sentence. You help her as she spells it out, moving one card from the top to the bottom for every letter.

"I don't know how that helps us find your card, but it sure is fun, isn't it? Please hold out the packet."

Rest your hand on the packet for a moment and perhaps murmur an incantation, like, "This better work or I'm sunk." (This provides a reason for the trick to work. Unbeknownst to one and all, you—you slick one—*could have* done something sneaky while your hand rested on the cards.)

"Beatrice, you strike me as a very magical person. Maybe you can find your own card...with the cards face down. Let's try. Just deal the top card onto the table. Put the next card on the bottom of the deck. Put the next card onto the table, and the next on the bottom of the deck." Have her continue until she holds only one card. Don't let her turn the card over just yet. "There's no way in the world that *I* could find your card; let's see how *you* did."

She did perfectly.

"You know what, Beatrice? I think magic *is* your business."

Note

If a spectator could remember exactly what you did, he could do the trick himself. But the steps are sufficiently complicated to make this unlikely.

GENERAL TRICKS

POISON PERSONALITY

Here we have one of the more amusing Bob Hummer tricks. I don't know if he originally intended that it be amusing, but that's the way I see it. I've made a few changes and have emphasized the humorous aspects.

Dolores is a firm believer in almost every kind of fortune-telling, so she'd be the perfect subject for this stunt. "Dolores, I'd like to test your personality, using this deck of cards." Hand her the deck. "For this to work, you must handle the deck, of course. Just spread the cards face up on the table."

When she finishes, say, "Now pick out any eight cards that you wish. Just take them right out of the spread."

After she removes the eight cards, pick up the rest of the deck and set it aside. Look at the eight cards and make some comments about a few of them. Here are some possibilities.

"You picked out a 7. This means you believe very much in luck."

"Here's a queen. You have a very good female friend."

"Ah, a king (or jack). You're attracted to a particular male."

"The ten of diamonds. This means you're very interested in jewelry."

You can probably make up even better lies.

After several comments, turn the cards face down. "But, Dolores, these cards can reveal much more about you, based on how many you would choose to turn face up." There are five different personalities: a 4-4 personality, a 5-3 personality, a 6-2 personality, a 7-1 personality, and an 8-zero personality.

"The 4-4 personality is where you have four cards face up and four cards face down. This indicates a neutral person, someone who doesn't have strong opinions."

"The 6-2 personality is a hard worker, who still takes the time to enjoy and to share with others."

"The 8-0 personality is totally obsessed, either with work or idleness. This type may find enormous success but pays a tremendous price in the lack of personal relationships."

"The 7-1 personality is the best of all: diligent, hardworking, loving, self-sacrificing—I could go on for hours." Pause. "I'm a 7-1."

"The worst personality is the 5-3—5 cards facing one way, and 3 cards facing the other. Through scientific research, we've determined that a 5-3 is totally despicable, lazy, incompetent, rude—everything that the world despises."

Hold the packet in your left hand. Say to Dolores, "I'd like you to stand facing the group." As you say this, take her hand in your right hand and move her so that she's in front of you. "Please put your hands behind your back and take these cards." While you are hidden from the group, turn the top card of the packet face up. Immediately place the packet into one of her hands.

Provide the following directions, with suitable pauses:

"Please mix the cards up. Turn over the top two cards. Mix the cards again. Turn over the top two cards. Continue doing this for as long as you wish."

When she is done, tell her, "You can continue mixing and turning over if you want to." When she's finally satisfied, have her bring the cards forward.

Fan through the cards so that all can see. Slowly count the face-up and face-down cards. "Good heavens! she's a 5-3. I can't believe this. Dolores seems so nice." Pause. "I'm certainly glad that *I'm* not a 5-3. How about the rest of you? Yeah, we're all glad that *we're* not 5-3's."

It's a good idea to have at least two other people try the personality test. They pick out eight cards, and you discuss the choices briefly. Then you turn over a card on top as you give them the cards, making sure that both of them turn out to be 5-3's (or, rarely, a 7-1).

Then: "I don't think *everyone* here is a 5-3." Have someone else pick out eight cards; you discuss the cards briefly. Then simply have her pick up the cards and put them behind her back. The result will be that the face-up and face-down cards will both be an even number. Occasionally, the cards will produce 8-0.

You can have considerable fun with this as you have some of the finest persons in the world end up as 5-3's.

Notes

(1) Occasionally, it will turn out that the spectator is a 7-1. When this happens, you might say, "Wow! so you're a 7-1, too. Like me, you're practically perfect. I'll bet we're the only 7-1's here."

(2) The persons who decide to try out the experiment on their own will be neither a 5-3 nor a 7-1. Without a card turned over at the beginning, the result will always be either 4-4, 6-2, or (rarely) 8-0.

(3) Perhaps Dolores would like to try it again. If so, she'll discover that the first result was totally wrong, and you can celebrate with her the fact that she's not as bad as everyone thought she was.

(4) You can have fun defining the 5-3 personality, based on the spectator who is assisting you. You can list things that have nothing to do with her actual personality, or things that are right on the money. Needless to say, you don't want to go overboard so that your assistant's feelings are hurt.

(5) This trick can also be performed when both you and your assistant are seated across from each other at a table. Hand her the eight cards under the table, turning over the top card once you get both hands under the table. She then does the two-card turnover and the mixing beneath the table.

FIVE-CARD TURNABOUT

Five cards, ace through 5, are dealt out in order. But with a wave of the hand, you cause them to reverse their order. Milt Kort did not invent the trick, but he developed much of the handling and the basic logic behind it.

Remove from the deck these cards: AD, 2D, 3D, 4D, 5D. (Clearly, any suit will do.) As you toss the cards face up onto the table, say, "I have trouble understanding a weird shuffle I heard about. Maybe you can help me."

Pick up the ace and place it face up in your hand. On top of it, place the face-up 5. Follow this with the 2, the 4, and the 3. When you turn the packet face down, they will be in this order, from the top: A, 5, 2, 4, 3. It's easy to remember because the order is logical:

Rather than consider the ace as a high card, think of it as a one. The order then goes low to high, low to high, and then middle. First , you go lowest to highest (A to 5), then from second lowest to second highest (2 to 4), and finally to the middle (3).

Turn the packet face down. "Now I'll show you the weird shuffle I mentioned." Start fanning through the cards from top to the bottom. As you do this, you perform an abbreviated version of the up-and-down shuffle. (See *The Up-and-Down Shuffle*, page 11.) The first card goes up, the second down, and so forth. You end up with two cards sticking out the bottom of the packet. These two are stripped out by the right hand and placed on top of the packet. From the top down, the cards now run 5, 4, A, 2, 3.

Repeat this "shuffle" three times (four times in all); the cards are now in the same position as when you started. As you repeat this up-down shuffle, keep repeating, "I don't know if I'm mixing these up or sorting them out."

When you're finished, add, "This is the strangest shuffle."

Deal the top card face down onto the table. Place the next card under the packet. Deal the next card to the right of the first card on the table. The next card goes to the bottom of the packet. Continue until all five cards are in a row on the table. Turn them over, showing that they run in order from your left to right.

Gather up the cards one by one, placing them face up in your left hand. This time, you pick up the cards in their natural order, starting with the ace, following with the 2, and so on. *Except* that you pick up the 5 third and the 3 last. In other words, as you pick up the cards, you exchange the positions of the 5 and 3. So, when you turn the pile face down, the cards will run from the top A, 2, 5, 4, 3.

As you gather up the cards, say, "I would love that shuffle if only it were consistent. But when I do it, I have no idea of what's going to happen." By this time the cards should have been gathered and turned face down.

You again perform your weird "shuffle." Now, however, you do it only three times. And don't forget to say, each time, "I don't know if I'm mixing these up or sorting them out." After three "shuffles," this will be the order of the cards: 5, A, 2, 4, 3.

At the end of this third up-and-down shuffle, you're holding two cards at the sides in your right hand. When you place the two cards on top, get a small break below them with the tip of your left little finger. This is by way of preparation for a double-lift. You will find the basic move under *When Putting Cards on Top of the Deck*, page 9. You should probably check it out before proceeding with this variation.

As described, you obtain a break beneath the top two cards with your left little finger. Your left thumb is resting on the left side of the deck. With the palm-down right hand, you grip the packet on the ends, near the right side. The first finger is on top, the second finger grips the cards at the outer end; the thumb, at the inner end, takes over the break held by your left little finger (Illus. 42).

Slide your right hand to the left side of the packet; the right thumb retains and expands the break below the top two cards (Illus. 43). Display the ace by swinging the top two cards in an

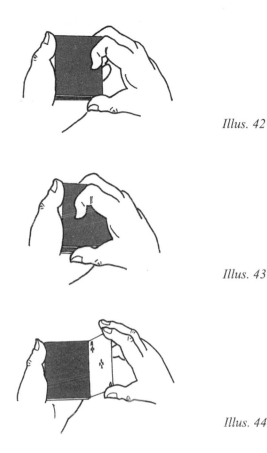

Illus. 42

Illus. 43

Illus. 44

arc to the right, as though opening the back cover of a book (Illus. 44). Say, "Ace," as you return the double-card to its original face-down position. Deal the top card (the 5) face down onto the table. Just as you did before, move the new top card to the bottom of the packet.

Spread the four cards to show that everything is fair and aboveboard. Actually, you are just making it easier to once more get a break beneath the top two cards with your left little finger. Close up the cards. Once more, perform the double-lift as described above. This time, you display the 2. Return the double-card to its original face-down position, saying, "Two." Deal the top card (the 4) face down onto the table, to your right of the first card. Move the new top card to the bottom of the packet.

To be consistent, spread the three remaining cards, showing them. Close them up. Display the 3 in precisely the same manner as you did the first two cards. Turn it face down onto the packet, saying, "Three." Deal it onto the table to the right of the other two cards.

You are now holding two cards. Move the top one below the other one. Make a show of spreading the two cards. Put the top one on the table to the right of the other cards, saying, "Four." Place the last one down to the right of all, saying, "Five."

You now use some "time misdirection." Address one of the group, "Do you think you could do that weird shuffle?" Whatever the answer, say, "Maybe you could; I don't know. Sometimes there's something magical about it. Take a look at what happens." Point to the table. "I put these down in order-ace, two, three, four, five. Now look at them."

Starting at your left, turn the cards over, showing them to be in reverse order: 5, 4, 3, 2, ace.

Note

Instead of performing the double-lift as described above, you may follow the exact procedure described in *An Easy Double-Lift*, page 13. Or, of course, you may substitute any double-lift you're familiar with.

FIVE CHOICE CARDS

Alex Elmsley, one of the all-time great innovators in card magic, came up with this unique approach to a standard trick. I have made some slight changes.

Fan through the face-up deck, saying, "Let's see, we'll need five red and five black cards."

Therefore, you remove ten cards from the deck—five red, five black. You remove them one at a time, placing them into a face-up pile on the table in a particular order. The order is easy to remember. You start with a pair of alternating colors. Let's say you place a red card down face up. On top of it, you must place a black card. So face up on the table, you have: **R-B**.

The next four pairs will each contain a red and a black, but each will begin with the same color as the last card placed down. In this instance, the last card placed down was a black. Therefore, the next card you place down must also be a black. And it is followed by a red: **R-B B-R**.

The next pair? You've already guessed. It begins with a red. Thus: **R-B B-R R-B**.

All five pairs will be as follows: **R-B B-R R-B B-R R-B**.

So you will either have the above order: **R B B R R B B R R B**. Or you will have this order: **B R R B B R R B B R**.

Either order will do just fine.

Pick up the pile of cards and turn it face down.

Raymond has agreed to assist you, so you must explain, "Raymond, you'll choose five of these cards." Take off the top card. "If you choose this card, it goes onto the table." Deal it onto the table, but keep your grip on it.

Replace it on top of the packet, still retaining your grip.

"If you don't choose the top card, it goes on the bottom." Move the card to the bottom, and then back to the top.

"Let's mix the cards up a bit so that neither of us knows which is where." You're about to give the packet an up-and-down shuffle. (See *The Up-and-Down Shuffle*, page 11.) But first, ask Raymond, "Should the first card go up or go down?" Do as he indicates; then complete the up-and-down portion of the shuffle. Strip out the lower packet. "Should this packet go on top of the other packet or below it?" Do as he indicates.

Place the packet onto the table. "You'd better give them a cut, Raymond." The cards are given as many complete cuts as desired.

Pick up the packet, saying, "I'd better mix them some more." Give the packet another up-and-down shuffle, giving Raymond the same choices as before.

It seems impossible but the top five cards are all of the same color, and, of course, so are the bottom five cards.

Put the cards behind your back. Bring the top one forward, holding it face down. "Raymond, do you want this one, or not?" If he wants it, place it onto the table (or on his hand). In the latter instance, say, "Don't peek."

If the card is rejected, place it back on top. Fiddle around a bit and bring out the same card. (Presumably, you've placed it on the bottom.)

Continue like this until Raymond has chosen five cards.

"Every once in a blue moon, Raymond, a spectator proves that he has exceptional ESP by choosing cards that are all the same color. Let's see what you have?"

He turns his cards over. Sure enough, he has chosen all of the same color. You bring the other cards forward. And, of course, you have all of the other color.

Notes

(1) You might do the trick this way. Sneak a peek at the bottom card of the packet after you perform the last up-and-down shuffle. The bottom five cards will all be of the same color. Ask Raymond, "Which do you prefer, Raymond—red or black?" Suppose he says red. If the bottom card was red, you let him choose from the bottom five cards. If it was black, you let him choose from the top five cards.

At the end, express surprise at his ability to choose the exact color that he wanted.

(2) How do you end up with the blacks and reds separated? Simple, really. After the first up-and-down shuffle, the colors alternate. The complete cuts do not affect this order. And the next up-and-down shuffle separates the blacks and reds.

(3) The cards *cannot* be cut before you make your first up-and-down shuffle. This will destroy the proper order.

CLOCK TRICKS

THE CLOCK STRIKES AGAIN

This trick, my invention, is colorful, quick, and extremely puzzling. Spectators seem to enjoy tricks in which you lay out cards in a clock-formation.

Annie needs to know everything, so explain to her, "I'll need 11 spot cards to make up a clock. You'll furnish the 12th card."

Without letting the spectators see the cards, find a 2 of any suit and place it face down on the table. Place on top of it a face-down 4. Follow this with a 6, an 8, and a 10. Next comes an ace, followed by a 3, a 5, a 7, a 9, and another 5.

So from the bottom up, you have 2, 4, 6, 8, 10, A, 3, 5, 7, 9, 5. This should be easy enough to remember. First come the even spot cards from low to high, followed by the odd spot cards from low to high, and then an extra 5. The suits don't matter.

Hand Annie the rest of the deck. "Please pick out any face card." You take it from her, announce its name, and place it face down on top of the packet. Give the packet a cut. Have Annie cut the cards. Other spectators may cut as well. When they are satisfied, take the cards back.

At this point, you may decide to try out some patter provided by Wally Wilson: "*Tempus fugit*, Latin for 'time flies,' is found on many timepieces. You may have heard the expression that 'time flies like an arrow,' or that 'fruit flies like rotten bananas.' Let's see if the seconds will fly by as we try to end up with the face card you selected."

Deal the cards *clockwise* into a face-down circle. "This is a clock. But we're not going to know which way the clock is facing until someone chooses a 12 o'clock card." Have Annie pick a 12 o'clock card. You move it slightly out of line. "Now please pick a time. We're going to hope for very good luck now."

Annie picks a time. You start with one o'clock and, touching each card in order, count to the selected time. Turn this card face up. If it turns out to be the face card, quit; you've just performed a spectacular trick. Chances are rather strong, however, that she'll pick a spot card.

You say, "You have chosen the 12 o'clock card without any help from me, and you've selected a time. The cards were cut several times. Despite all this, I have a strong feeling that you'll find it extremely difficult to find the face card you selected. In fact, you might just find it last."

Explain that, starting with the next card in order, she is to count clockwise, moving the number of cards indicated by the value shown on her selection. For example, suppose Annie picks 3 o'clock; you count to this time and turn over the card at 3 o'clock. Let's suppose that it's a 6. She starts with the next card, the one which stands for 4 o'clock, and counts that as 1. She counts to 6, touching a succeeding card for each count, landing on the card at 9 o'clock. She turns this card over. (It will be a 5.) Starting with the next card and moving clockwise, she counts five cards, turning over the fifth card. She continues in this manner until only one card remains face down.

"Only one card remains—the face card which you chose." Turn the face card over and place it face up in the middle of the circle.

After everyone has had a chance to see the display, gather up the cards. You don't want the group to have a chance to study the pattern. Don't hurry, but don't dally either.

Notes

(1) You may want to speed the trick up by counting and turning over the cards yourself.

(2) I've never had a spectator figure out the trick. Still, if you're afraid that a brilliant friend might discern the pattern, you might try this: After the spectator turns over his first card, announce the value and give your speech

about what you hope will happen. Then fan through the face-up deck to a face card. Cut the cards so that this becomes the bottom card of the deck. This sends all the spot cards below the face card to the top of the deck, thus making it easier to find succeeding face cards. Take the face card and place it face up on top of the spectator's face-up card. "I'm going to cover your choice with a face card for luck. If I'm right, when you turn over your last card, we'll have all face cards."

When the spectator counts to his next card, you fan through to the next face card and cut the cards so that it becomes the bottom card of the deck. (You do this for each succeeding face card.) This face card goes face up on the card he counted to. You continue on. Eventually all the cards are covered with face cards and one card is face down: the face card he chose at the beginning.

HICKORY-DICKORY-DOCK

I consulted my friends Wally Wilson and Milt Kort about the possibility of improving the above trick. They came up with a clever adaptation of an old principle in which you always end up with the bottom card of 11 cards. Wally figured that the principle could easily be adapted to a clock trick, and Milt verified this.

Using their idea, I worked out a way to locate a selected card. Thus, two great minds and my mind combine to offer this colorful, effective trick.

Fan through the deck and remove the QS. Toss it onto the table face up. "Let's try an experiment in which we'll use some cards to form a clock. But first: As you know, all women have mysterious powers, and queens have more than most. In the deck of cards, the queen of spades has more power than any other card. Naturally, she'll serve as 12 o'clock, the highest number. And just maybe, she'll help bring about a magical result."

You'll need someone who's fairly adept with cards to assist you, so ask Fred to help out.

Casually count off 11 cards and hand them to him. "Fred, I'd like you to mix those cards thoroughly. When you're satisfied, look at the bottom card and remember it. You may show it to others so they can share the fun."

After he finishes, continue: "Now we want that card mixed in among the others, so you get a choice. Do you want to do the down-under shuffle, or the under-down shuffle?"

If you say this fast enough, Fred is bound to be confused. So explain slowly: "If you choose the down-under shuffle, you place the first card down and put the next card under the packet. The next card goes down, and the next one under the packet, until all the cards are on the table.

"If you choose the under-down shuffle, the first card goes under the packet and the next one onto the table, the next one under the packet, and the next one onto the table, until all the cards are on the table.

"Either way, you'll give the cards two shuffles of the same sort. So which do you prefer, down-under or under-down?"

Make sure he understands. Have him perform one of the two types of shuffles. He then picks up the cards and does the same kind of shuffle again. His chosen card is now either on the top or bottom of the pile of 11 cards. It's easy to remember which. If he performed two *under*-down deals, his card is *under*; that is, it's on the bottom. Otherwise, it's on top.

You take the cards from Fred and deal them face down into a clock formation, starting from the face-up QS, which is at 12 o'clock. If his card is on the bottom (that is, he performed the *under*-down shuffles), you start at 1 o'clock and deal around to 11 o'clock. If his card is on top, you start at 11 o'clock and deal backward to 1 o'clock. Clearly, in either instance, the chosen card is at 11 o'clock. You do *not* say the numbers aloud as you place the cards down.

"Pick any time you wish," you say to Fred. In the unlikely

event that he says 11, say, "Are you sure you want that? You can choose any time at all." He'll probably stick with his choice. Touch the card at one o'clock, saying, "One." Continue around the circle, stating each number as you touch the appropriate card. After landing on 11, say, "What was the name of your chosen card?" He names it. Turn over the card at 11 o'clock. Sure enough, it's the chosen one. Just another of your many miracles.

But Fred is much more likely to name some other number. "We'll count that number out again and again, eliminating one card each time by turning it face up. If we're in luck, your chosen card will be the last one eliminated." Point to the face-up QS. "As you can see, the queen of spades is already eliminated, so we'll not use her at all in the counting. Besides, she'd be insulted. Everyone knows you can't count on a queen." Pause, providing everyone the chance to give you an appropriate dirty look. "If you want to, Fred, you can change your mind and choose another time."

It really doesn't matter. The 11th card will be the last one eliminated, regardless.

Let's say that Fred chooses 5 o'clock. Move the QS well outside the circle so that you don't mistakenly count it (Illus. 45). Then count aloud from 1 o'clock to 5 o'clock, touching the appropriate cards as you go. Turn the card at 5 o'clock face up.

Illus. 45

Start with the next card, the one at 6 o'clock, and count to 5 aloud once more, moving clockwise and touching one card for each number. You land on 10 o'clock. Turn that card face up.

Start with the card at 11 o'clock and count off 5 again, making sure you *don't* count the QS. You land at the card at 4 o'clock. Turn it face up.

Continue on, remembering this: *Count every card, whether it be face up or face down.* The obvious exception is the QS, which is never counted.

Eventually, only one card is face down. Ask Fred to name his selection. He does. Sure enough, his chosen card is the last one to be eliminated.

Note

In this trick, you always end up with the 11th card. If you make a circle of 13 cards, you'll end up with the 13th card. In fact, if you make a circle of any *prime number* of cards and follow the procedure, you'll end up with the card at the prime number. A prime number is any number that can't be divided evenly by any numbers other than itself or the number 1. Examples: 1, 2, 3, 5, 7, 11, 13, 17, 19, 23, 29, etc.

MY TIME IS YOUR TIME

Wally Wilson showed me yet another clock trick. This one is extraordinarily deceptive.

Start by handing Jack the deck and asking him to give it a shuffle. When he's done, say, "It's no secret, Jack, that the number 12 is quite significant. For instance, there are the 12 signs of the Zodiac, the 12 months in a year, the 12 hours shown on the clock, and so on. So, please count off 12 cards into a pile."

After he does so, take the rest of the deck from him. "Please pick up your 12 cards, Jack."

You have placed the remainder of the deck into your left hand, preparatory to making an overhand shuffle. As Jack picks up his cards, you let the deck tilt slightly back toward the palm of your left hand (Illus. 46). Casually look down at your hands, sneaking a peek at the bottom card of the deck.

Illus. 46

This is important: Begin to give the cards an overhand shuffle *before* you say, "Shuffle your cards like this."

Jack shuffles his packet. You complete your overhand shuffle by shuffling off the last several cards individually, thus bringing the card you peeked at to the top of the deck.

(You must know the name of the top card of those you're holding. Clearly, any other sneaky way you want to do it is just fine.)

Set your cards onto the table. Avert your head and tell Jack, "Please cut off some of your cards and put them into your pocket. But don't pay attention to the number as you do this."

When he's done, say, "Put the rest of your cards on top of the deck and even up the deck."

You once more face the group.

"Neither of us knows how many cards you have in your pocket, right? Now I'd like you to pick up the deck and count out 12 cards, dealing them into a pile."

He does this.

"Set the rest of the deck aside. Pick up the pile of 12 cards and deal it out, forming a clock. The first card will be at one o'clock, and the last will be at 12 o'clock."

The clock has been formed. Move the card marking 12 o'clock an inch or two out of line as you comment, "So this is 12 o'clock."

Turn away. "I'd like you to take those cards from your pocket, Jack, and count them. But don't tell me the number."

He counts the cards.

"You have your number? Look at the card that lies at that time. For example, if you had four cards in your pocket, you'd look at the card that lies at four o'clock. Show the card around and then replace it face down. When you're done, put the cards that you had in your pocket back on top of the deck."

You turn back and reveal the chosen card any way you wish.

Remember that card you peeked at? Well, that's the one he chose. You can have him gather up all the cards and shuffle them. Then you can go through the deck and locate the card, or else read the spectator's mind.

My favorite conclusion is this: Before I turn back, I have the spectator gather up all the cards and shuffle them. When I face the group, I take the deck, riffle the ends a few times, and then rub it against my wristwatch.

"Since you used a clock in choosing a card, maybe my time-piece will help me identify it." I set the deck onto the table.

I hold my wristwatch to my ear and listen to it as it slowly gives me the color, the suit, and the value of the selected card.

Books by Bob Longe
Card Tricks Galore
Easy Card Tricks
Easy Magic Tricks
Great Card Tricks
Little Giant Encyclopedia of Magic
Magic Math Book
Mystifying Card Tricks
101 Amazing Card Tricks
World's Best Card Tricks
World's Best Coin Tricks
World's Greatest Card Tricks

MASTERY LEVELS CHART & INDEX